Congrats on Your Engagement

Letters to Tiffany

Neysa E. Taylor

Congrats on your Engagement

Letters to Tiffany

Neysa E. Taylor

CONGRATS ON YOUR ENGAGEMENT: Letters to Tiffany

© 2018 by Neysa E. Taylor

ISBN: 978-0692122471

NewSeason Books and Media
PO Box 1403
Havertown, PA 19083
www.nsbooksandmedia.com
newseasonbooks@gmail.com

All rights reserved. No part of this book may be reproduced in any form or by any means including electronic, mechanical or photocopying or stored in a retrieval system without permission in writing from the publisher except by a reviewer who may quote brief passages to be included in a review.

Table of Contents

Introduction 1

1 Proverbs 31 The Standard for a Woman of God 5
2 Clark Kent v. Superman.. 17
3 Dollars and *Cents*-ability 29
4 Praise and Worship 41
5 Learning to Survive the Storms 51
6 Circle of Friends 63
7 Family Matters 71
8 Forbidden Fruit 79
9 Sexual Healing... 87
10 Expanding the Family Tree 95
11 Write the Vision and Make It Plain 105
12 What's Next?... 113

Acknowledgments.. 117
My Prayer... 121

Introduction

Whenever people ask me about marriage, I tell them it is the hardest, most wonderful thing in the world. According to Pinterest (that's a legitimate source, right?), marriage is giving someone your heart and praying they don't drop it. While that train of thinking may give hope to many folks, it is also seriously flawed. You idolize your spouse when you first get married. You think, *This is the one person in the world who will never let me down.* But that is unrealistic. Spouses make mistakes. Some make small mistakes - like forgetting your birthday. Others make HUGE mistakes - like adultery. You should know going in that your spouse will make mistakes (Did you see that "s" on mistakes? Yep, that means it's plural.), and you will, too. But no one thinks of mistakes when you get a brand new diamond on her left hand.

    I learned about the true meaning of marriage when my marriage endured some major turbulence. After I sat still and dealt with the pain, I felt God wanted me to share my story. For years I heard Him say, "Write it down." At times I would start writing a blog, then stop when things got bumpy. I would start again. Then stop again. People would encourage me, and I would stop. It seemed like each time I picked up a pen, the storm would rage again. Finally, I decided to just forget it. Not only did I quit writing about marriage, I was done with writing altogether.

All of that changed when I had a business trip to Atlanta. During that trip, I had a wonderful brunch to catch up with my friend and soror Dr. Carolyn Hall. I must digress here and mention that Dr. Hall is also a professor, minister, author, and great woman of God. She's also a wonderful dancer and hilariously funny! After a lovely brunch at a quaint family-owned spot, Dr. Hall read the heck out of me. (Please note in this context, "reading" is the act of looking inside of you and telling you exactly what the Holy Spirit has instructed her to share.) To put it succinctly, she asked me when was I going to do what the Father told me to do? She added that people are waiting on me to write my story so that they can see what God can do in a marriage.

When I left Georgia, those words stuck with me. From time to time, I would think about what Carolyn said to me. It would play over and over in my mind and in my heart. But I didn't write anything. Fast forward a few months and one of my dearest friends, Tiffany, got engaged! Her boyfriend surprised her, dropped on one knee and popped the question on Tiffany's birthday. How sweet is that?! Tears of joy and much laughter celebrated that timeless moment. Who doesn't love love and the prospect of a wedding? The day after the proposal, I thought, *Wow, there is so much that I want to tell her about marriage.* I quickly shot down the idea because who was I to tell her about marriage? I'm not an authority. I'm not a Ph.D. I'm not a pastor. I know Tiff's got this. She's smart. She's an adult and knows what she is doing. But this is new territory for her - wife territory. I know this area. That's when I thought, *Who better to share with her about marriage than me?* I've been through the marriage fire and made tons of mistakes - some of which I am still paying for today. So who better than me to tell her what not to do, what to look out for and which minefields to avoid? I've been emotionally bruised, battered and blown to pieces, and I've done the same to my husband - but despite all of our dysfunction, our marriage is still standing (Thank you, Jesus!).

So I decided to share my "wisdom" with Tiffany. I wrote down all of the things that I wish I'd known before I got married. Add to that all of the things that I've learned during my marriage and ooo-weee, the pages just started filling up. So that's what you have here: basically, Neysa's mistakes and how to avoid them. And because I shared them with Tiffany, you get to benefit from it as well. I'm sure Tiffany won't mind.

1

Proverbs 31
The Standard for a Woman of God

Hey there, bride-to-be!

Let me first say. congrats on your upcoming nuptials! I know how exciting a time like this can be. You are probably up to your ears in white dresses, veils, beautiful shoes, and the hope of dancing the night away. I'm sure your days are filled with cake tasting and looking at reception venues. Don't stress about it! I am sure it will all be beautiful.

As a woman who has been in the marriage trenches for a minute, I wanted to write you a letter (or twenty) to help you avoid the mistakes I made throughout my union. I promise you that in writing this letter my goal is not to squash your joy and bubbly feelings. I want to make sure that you are as prepared for marriage as you are for the wedding.

So let's put all of this wife business in context. Take a minute and read Psalm 31:10-31:

Neysa E. Taylor

[b]*A wife of noble character who can find?*
She is worth far more than rubies.
¹¹ *Her husband has full confidence in her*
and lacks nothing of value.
¹² *She brings him good, not harm,*
all the days of her life.
¹³ *She selects wool and flax*
and works with eager hands.
¹⁴ *She is like the merchant ships,*
bringing her food from afar.
¹⁵ *She gets up while it is still night;*
she provides food for her family
and portions for her female servants.
¹⁶ *She considers a field and buys it;*
out of her earnings she plants a vineyard.
¹⁷ *She sets about her work vigorously;*
her arms are strong for her tasks.
¹⁸ *She sees that her trading is profitable,*
and her lamp does not go out at night.
¹⁹ *In her hand she holds the distaff*
and grasps the spindle with her fingers.
²⁰ *She opens her arms to the poor*
and extends her hands to the needy.
²¹ *When it snows, she has no fear for her household;*
for all of them are clothed in scarlet.
²² *She makes coverings for her bed;*
she is clothed in fine linen and purple.
²³ *Her husband is respected at the city gate,*
where he takes his seat among the elders of the land.
²⁴ *She makes linen garments and sells them,*
and supplies the merchants with sashes.
²⁵ *She is clothed with strength and dignity;*
she can laugh at the days to come.
²⁶ *She speaks with wisdom,*
and faithful instruction is on her tongue.

> ²⁷ *She watches over the affairs of her household*
> *and does not eat the bread of idleness.*
> ²⁸ *Her children arise and call her blessed;*
> *her husband also, and he praises her:*
> ²⁹ *"Many women do noble things,*
> *but you surpass them all."*
> ³⁰ *Charm is deceptive, and beauty is fleeting;*
> *but a woman who fears the* LORD *is to be praised.*
> ³¹ *Honor her for all that her hands have done,*
> *and let her works bring her praise at the city gate.*

Have you ever really read Proverbs 31 in its entirety? That chick is bad! Awesome! She is doing a whole lot. Think about it. Verse 15 says she gets up at the crack of dawn to feed her family. She has a job (v.16), does community service (v.20), and is a great parent (v. 21). She also does housework (v. 22) and has multiple streams of income (v. 24). How many hours are in her day? I am tired just thinking about it. But that is the standard that a Godly wife is supposed to live up to and something we should strive to attain.

> **Do you know the difference between a Godly wife and a *Stepford* wife? These terms are not interchangeable. One is the standard we should strive for and one we should avoid.**

Notice that I called her a Godly wife not a perfect wife. Too often women get engaged and become *Stepford* wives. You know, the ring goes on and suddenly they become a caricature of what they think a wife should be. They immediately start taking on this persona of Claire Huxtable or Donna Reed. We attempt to embody how Hollywood tells us a wife should act.

I know I did it. When my husband Chris and I first moved in together, I became Little Suzy Homemaker. I wanted to attend to his every need before he ever thought of it. Do you remember the scene in *Coming to America* when Prince Hakeem meets his betrothed played by the lovely Vanessa Bell Calloway? His bride-to-be had been conditioned to serve him so well that she was brainless. When Prince Hakeem asked her to list her favorite things, all she could say was "Whatever you like." I was the same way. Chris thought I was awesome but I wasn't *authentic*. Not only was it not authentic, it wasn't sustainable. You cannot keep up a false version of yourself forever. Having a marriage that is based on falsehoods and being inauthentic will *kill* you. It will suck the life right out of you.

But here's some good news: you don't have to put on a façade because he chose you!

Reflection

Before we go any further, let's pause for a bit of reflection. Surely you didn't think I was going to just write these letters and not give you any homework? Take a moment and answer a few questions about yourself.

1. **Who are you?** Not who are you at work or at church, but who are you when you are alone in your house on a Friday night? Who are you when no one is watching?
2. **Does your beloved know this person?** Did he propose to your PR agent or your core?
3. **What does being a "wife" mean to you?** What traits does a wife embody? Do you meet these traits? Do you believe that any of the traits you listed will be hard for you to attain?

Let me tell you why answering those questions is crucial. You have decided to merge your life with another human being. This isn't just seeing your boo-thang on a Friday night after you've had two hours to shave your legs and apply your face. This person will see you at your best. They will see the wedding day you — when you are slaying all of us as you walk down the aisle. But they will also see the stomach-flu you, the morning breath you, and the constipated you. Trust me, those yous are not pretty. Your spouse will see you when everything is going right and your heart is full, but they will also see you at your most broken. You have to possess great knowledge of self and be authentic as you prepare to become a wife.

He Loves You Right Now

Look down at your left hand. See that piece of jewelry sitting there on your ring finger? Do you think that was the only ring in the store? It probably wasn't. While I wasn't shopping with your fiancé, I am sure there were rows and rows of engagement rings to choose from at the jewelry store. There are also hundreds of jewelry stores across the city. But look at your hand again. There was something so special about this ring that he selected it for you to wear as your engagement ring.

Guess what? The same goes for you. He asked you to marry him. In a field full of women, he chose you. He didn't ask Halle Berry or Taylor Swift. He. Asked. You. That means that right now, just as you are, he loves you. My pastor, Bishop Joseph Warren Walker III of Mount Zion Baptist Church, says that men get engaged hoping you don't change. But it seems that women get married thinking everything is changing. That difference in perspective is a doozie. Men put a ring on your finger hoping to freeze time like Hans Solo when he was encased in carbonite. (Out of everything I've ever written, I think that last line made my hubs the happiest). Women get the ring and feel like they are being immediately promoted to a new level. Some want to start changing every single thing. Like the shirt their boyfriend wore last week isn't really a fiance' shirt because in their newly engaged mind fiances wear collared shirts.

Don't be this chick.

While change is inevitable, being engaged means that right now you are exactly what he wants. Take comfort in the fact that *he loves you*.

***

Even if you aren't a member of the Bey Hive, you've probably heard of a Beyoncé song entitled "Flaws and All." In this ballad she sings "I don't know why you love me/and that's why I love you/You catch me when I fall/Accept me flaws and all/And that's why I love you." That is a great feeling. Someone who loves you when you have a zit, bad breath, or are bloated. Your fiancé should be someone who loves you unconditionally. Unconditional love is agape love. Agape love is the highest form of love. Of course, Christians get that agape love from Christ. Ephesians 5:25-33 reads:

> [25] *Husbands, love your wives, just as Christ loved the church and gave himself up for her* [26] *to make her holy, cleansing[a] her by the washing with water through the word,* [27] *and to present her to himself as a radiant church, without stain or wrinkle or any other blemish, but holy and blameless.* [28] *In this same way, husbands ought to love their wives as their own bodies. He who loves his wife loves himself.* [29] *After all, no one ever hated their own body, but they feed and care for their body, just as Christ does the church —* [30] *for we are members of his body.* [31] *"For this reason a*

man will leave his father and mother and be united to his wife, and the two will become one flesh."[b] *32 This is a profound mystery — but I am talking about Christ and the church. 33 However, each one of you also must love his wife as he loves himself, and the wife must respect her husband.*

If Christ is the standard for husbands, then that love should be amazing! It's sacrificial - there's no greater sacrifice than the one Jesus made for us - and it's unwavering. It's truly a "flaws and all" love, and you are blessed to have found it in your fiancé.

Engagement Is a Time of Preparation

So, I just spent the last few paragraphs telling you that your fiancé loves you and doesn't want you to change. Now, I'm going to tell you to prepare for change. I know, it's a contradiction but hey, that's life.

Your engagement is from the time you say "yes" until the moment you say "I do." This is your time to spiritually, mentally, and physically prepare yourself for marriage. Yep, you have to prepare for marriage on all levels. Your husband is a gift to you, and you are a gift to your husband. How you serve your husband is worship unto God. Now it's easy to say this while at the computer typing away, but it is true. You honor God by honoring your husband. This is even more true when he is on your last nerve. (Believe me, there will come a time when he will be tap dancing on your last nerve!)

When preparing for a wedding, many churches have a rule that a couple must do marriage counseling before they can rent the church. So people begrudgingly take marriage counseling classes for a few hours or a few weeks. But how long do you plan a wedding? Months? Years? People do marriage counseling for a few weeks and plan a wedding for months. That is backwards. Truth be told, I didn't even do that much marriage counseling before I got married, and my marriage suffered for it. The fact that Chris and I lived together before we got married made me believe that the act of getting married was simply a ceremony. I truly thought that living together was pretty much the same as getting married. In my mind, the wedding was just the icing on the cake. I was wrong, totally wrong. Did I mention that I was wrong? Because I was, you know, wrong.

Girl, don't be wrong. Be right.

> **Just like college is preparation for the working world, engagement is prep time for a marriage — not just a wedding.**

Strategic use of the engagement period is critical to the success of your marriage. Remember when you graduated from college? If you are like me, in the midst of the commencement celebration, it suddenly hit you that now the real work starts. College was just preparation for the real world. No more summer breaks, it was now time to get a *real* job. Engagement is basically college for marriage. It is a time to soak up all that you need to learn *before* you become his wife. This doesn't mean you will stop learning the minute that white dress hits the floor. It's just that this time is crunch time.

During this prep time, you have to prepare on every level, but most importantly the spiritual one. Now, I am not saying that you should start walking around the house speaking in tongues whenever your fiancé calls your name. I do mean you should be intentional about your time in prayer. Spend time daily in the Word and in prayer. As you are praying, ask God if this man is actually your husband. I know, I know! Stop the presses! You said "yes to the dress," so this man is going to be your hubs, but are you sure? Often we get caught up on being in love with being in love. Or we like the thought of winning a prize or being selected as wife material. Women feel that being engaged makes us special and a little better than the rest of the flock. It's like joining a secret club or sorority. But you need to pray and see if you are actually a match made in heaven or just a chick who likes jewelry on her left hand. Those are two very different things.

    The bottom line is that you have to prepare for marriage. Satan hates marriage. John 10:10 says "the thief comes to steal, kill, and destroy." Marriage is the foundation of the family, and family is the cornerstone of the kingdom of God. Satan hates anything that builds the kingdom. Know that the enemy will attack your marriage. As the old saying goes: an ounce of prevention is worth a pound of cure. Trust me. Believe me. You would rather do the work now than suffer the pain of a failed marriage.

Build a Temple

With all the foundation and cornerstone metaphors I'm using, you would think I was an architect. I'm not. But those construction analogies are great examples of what a marriage should be—a union firmly built on a strong foundation. So let's keep the engineering metaphor going and read the first two lines of 2 Chronicles 2: "[King] Solomon gave orders to build a temple for the Name of the Lord and a royal palace for himself."

I love this verse because while the focus is on building a temple, the kickback is that Solomon gets a royal palace as well. And Solomon didn't spare any expense. This was the G5 level of temples. So if the temple was going to be nice, you know the palace was going to be amazing!

This is how I envision marriage to be. A Christian marriage is a temple for God. Every day, every action works together to build a temple to God. The kickback is that by honoring God, you get to reap the benefits of a strong, healthy marriage. That is one heck of a benefit!

If you are thinking, "I'm getting married! I will have 80 years to build a temple," you are right. But your engagement period is a time for pouring the foundation. The foundation of a home determines if the home will not only stand but be strong enough to withstand storms. If your subfloor has termite-ridden beams, then your entire house will crumble. If you use bad drywall, your walls will become moldy and fall down. It's the same for your relationship. If you do not lay the right foundation, your relationship can (and will) fall apart. As I mentioned before, everything you do during this preparation period can help you build a strong foundation. I'm not telling you this because I did everything right. I am telling you this because I did everything wrong.

When the storms came in my marriage, I thought I could rationalize them away. I thought I could argue them away. I thought I could cry, kick, scream, move out, put him out, and a slew of other wrong answers. When it came down to it, the only thing I could do was pray. My relationship with God was *not* where it needed to be. I was ill equipped to handle this category 5 hurricane that was raging in my life. So before I could even focus on my marriage, I had to focus on Jesus and what He wanted me to do. I wasted years before I figured this out. YEARS, I tell you! But when I really said, "Ok, God, what do You want me to do?" I was able to see that Jesus needed *our* relationship to be better before I could even think about repairing my marriage.

Reflection

Time for more homework. Let's dig in to your vision for your future marriage.

1. Since the moment you said "yes" to the ring, have you thought about your wedding day? Have you mentally played through your dream day?
2. Have you given any thought to your dream marriage? Use your imagination and write down what your ideal marriage looks like, feels like, and sounds like?
3. How are you preparing for this future? Yes, I know you are reading these letters but be intentional about your preparation time.

Hey, friend, use these letters and learn from my mistakes. Don't spend all your time focused on dress fittings and menus. Wedding stuff is important but fleeting. Seriously, a wedding is approximately 1 hour with a four hour reception. So you plan for months for the first 5 *hours of your marriage.* That's it. Make sure you have also planned for the next 80 years. Focus on pouring a strong foundation upon which you will build your temple. You can either do the work now or pay for the cost of repairs later.

You got this!
Neysa

2

Clark Kent v. Superman

My happy bride-to-be,

Did you know I love superheroes? I do! Wonder Woman, Luke Cage, Batman, Black Panther, X-Men...I really love them all. There is something about a person with a secret identity and a cape that can have me glued to the TV for hours on end. Even if you aren't a superhero nerd like myself you've probably seen a Superman movie. I think I've seen them all, including most of the *Smallville* episodes. Each time I watch a Superman movie, I wonder about his relationship with Lois Lane. What if Clark Kent never became Superman? Does she only love Clark Kent because of his super potential? If he remained Clark, would Lois still love him? (I know, I know. I think too much.)

Many women love potential. We can go to Goodwill, see a shabby desk, and think, "With a little paint, this could be beautiful. This desk has potential." That is an awesome quality to have with interior design or when flipping houses. But when it comes to your spouse, only seeing potential is a problem.

While you can't solely focus on your fiancé's potential, you can't ignore it either. (Isn't that another contradiction?) You need to be aware of your future spouse's dreams and wants. You have to be able to see the core of his being and know how to nurture those seeds into fruition.

But here's something to consider: while you are nurturing those seeds, can you handle the work and uncertainty of changing seasons? No one ever wakes up and says, "Today, I shall step into my destiny." Well, maybe they do say it, but rarely is it that easy. Growth is accompanied by hard work, frustration, and discomfort. Can you love your spouse through transitional periods?

I know those are tough questions, so let's jump into it.

> **Do you love your fiancé, or do you love his potential? Those are not the same.**

Love Him Today

In the previous letter, I mentioned that your fiancé loves you *right now*. When you look at your left hand and see that ring sitting there, do you still have that warm, fuzzy feeling? Well, guess what? You have to do the same. You have to love him - all of him - *today*. A real estate investor can look at a home or a piece of property and think, *in 10-20 years, this is the area of town that will increase in value.* They will then purchase the property and hold onto it until they can get a return on their investment. Marriage is not a real estate venture. Real estate tycoons buy a property but normally don't live there every day. You are getting married. You will live with your spouse day in and day out. You can't wait for 10-20 years before you fully love him. According to McKinley-Irvin Family Law[1], the average length of a marriage that ends in divorce is eight years. So if you are waiting on a ten-year return on investment, you are going to be short by about two years. That's not going to work.

When Michelle Robinson met Barack Obama, he wasn't president of the United States. He was Barry from Hawaii. He wasn't wearing a presidential suit or standing at a podium leading the free world. He was in jeans and a T-shirt. She may have seen the potential of Barack, but she fell in love with Barry. While his career goals have obviously grown exponentially, Michelle Obama had to love flip-flop wearing Barry whether or not he ever transitioned into Barack.

It took me a while to learn this concept. I loved Chris (I still love Chris), but I'm extremely ambitious. I want to impact the world right now and always have a gazillion irons in the fire as I try to grow. Chris is a bit more turtle-ish. He prefers to slowly and cautiously try out new ideas. I wanted to be a power couple. To be the "it" couple. You know the Jay-Z and Beyoncé, the Will and Jada couple. I wanted to do really big things and have him make equally big moves. We'd take the world by storm! Basically, I wanted us to both be superheroes and fly around the world. I had to learn that Chris' dreams are his, and I can't achieve them for him. He has to step into his dream when he is ready to do so. I had to love Clark Kent and allow his Superman to develop when he was ready to fly.

---

[1] http://www.mckinleyirvin.com/Family-Law-Blog/2012/October/32-Shocking-Divorce-Statistics.aspx

Reflection

Yep, it is time. Ask yourself these questions:

1. Do you love your fiancé?
2. If time stopped right now, could you love this person?
3. If he never got a raise, can you love him?
4. If he wore this outfit for the next 80 years, could you love him?

These questions might sound trivial because no man is that stagnant, but they get to the core question of...**do you love this person now, just as they are, in this moment?** This is so important because we always think of life as flourishing. That point of view is optimistic and hopeful, but you have to be prepared for hard times, too. If you think where you are right now is basecamp, and it can only go up from here, let me introduce you to Job. I know you know the story of Job. Job was minding his own business when all hell broke loose in his world. (see Job 1:13) Well, just like things can get better, they can get worse, too. If you are only waiting on Superman to show up, what are you going to do if Clark Kent gets sick, loses a job, or gets injured? Can you love a broken Clark Kent? The vows that you will soon take say "for better or for worse." You have to truly love the person at their core to endure times of increase and times of lack.

Planting Seeds for the Future

You've answered the above questions and decided that you love your man. You LOVE him right now, right here, in this moment. Great! Now let's talk about his future. Before you give me the side-eye for contradicting myself (Get over it. I'll likely keep doing it), let me explain: You have to love him today, but you also have to nurture seeds for the future. This is vitally important because from the moment you say, "I Do," your futures are tied together.

Imagine a farmer in front of a vast vegetable garden. Do you take fertile ground, plant a few seeds, and then walk away, hoping for the best? Not if you want to eat, you don't. If you want a fruitful harvest, you water the seeds. Make sure they get enough sunlight. You protect the seeds even while they are dormant because you know that one day they will bear fruit. You must treat your fiancé the same way.

One of the most important ways you can protect and sow into your beloved's future is by guarding your mouth. I was (actually, I really still am) a person who likes to be blunt. I don't like to play with semantics or give anything the opportunity to be misconstrued. I'm a bit direct. But every good communicator knows that sharing a message is only part of the communication process. You must also deliver it in a way that is appropriate for the audience to which you are speaking. It's funny how we carefully craft our words at work or church, but at home we have no restraint. In the past, I would think, "Well, this is my safe place. They know what I mean and that I mean it in love." But nothing could be further from the truth. Your words mean more *because* they love you. Think about it this way: You are walking down the street and a stranger turns to you and says, "I really don't like you. We can't be friends." You will probably shrug it off and not care because you don't know this person. You place no value in them. But let your best friend come to you and say, "I really don't like you anymore. We can't be friends." You would be devastated. Tears may fall. You would wonder what you did and how you can make it right. The sentiment and word choice of both people was the same, but because of the value you placed on the person, the words felt different. If you haven't noticed, your fiancé places you in a place of importance in his life. He chose you to value. So choose your words carefully.

Proverbs 31:26 shares this about a noble wife: "She speaks with wisdom, and faithful instruction is on her tongue." A Godly wife knows when to speak to her hubs, how to speak to her hubs, and what to say to her hubs. That means she knows the time, the tone, and the text. She knows when to say it, what voice to use, and what words to say that will convey her point but not stir up strife. This is hard work for most women. I know this principle and I still verbally "vomit" from time to time. You know what I mean? I want to say something so badly that my mind is warring with my mouth. This especially happens when I am angry. I feel like I'm going to burst. Sometimes my mouth wins, and I say, "I probably shouldn't say this but…" That's how most of my outbursts start. If I'm honest about it, I rarely feel better about the situation after an outburst. I am constantly working in this area, but I have much more work to do.

We have to be careful about what we say because "the tongue has the power of life and death, and those who love it will eat its fruit" (Proverbs 18:21). We can build up our husbands or tear them down with our words. Imagine your fiancé standing in front of you holding an ornate crystal box. Every affirming word you say places a beautiful gem in the box. Every negative word you say about him takes jewels out of the box. Especially harsh fights make him drop the box, which causes it to shatter into a million, little pieces. You should always seek to fill the box up until it overflows because these are the words that he will use to later fuel his dreams. These are the words that he will use to carry him through the day when the world is on his shoulders and his back is against the wall. Your words are that important. That doesn't mean that if you have caused him to shatter his box in the past that it can't be rebuilt. It can. The box can be put back together through hard work. Each sliver must be painstakingly glued back together, and that process takes time. Trust me when I tell you that it is easier to think before you speak than it is to glue that love box back together.

<u>Reflection</u>

You knew I had to put a reflection in this section. Probably more for me than for you.

1. Do you have verbal diarrhea?
2. Do you words lean more toward cutting or healing?
3. If your mouth tends to run amuck from time to time, what practices can you put in place to make yourself pause before speaking?
4. Do you have this issue anywhere else like at work or school? If not, why?

Neysa E. Taylor

Change Gon' Come

We've all heard the Sam Cooke classic:

> "It's been too hard living, but I'm afraid to die
> 'Cause I don't know what's up there, beyond the sky
> It's been a long, a long time coming
> But I know a change gonna come, oh yes it will."

The only thing constant is change. If you are blessed to live more than two minutes, you have experienced change. Think about it. I'm 40+ years old as I write this book. I remember my uncle David giving me records to play on our large, buffet style record player. Later, as a pre-teen, I remember the Christmas I received my first Walkman that played cassette tapes. I blasted "Purple Rain" all of the time! After that, my mom purchased a small double cassette stereo for my room. I thought I was jamming because I could dub a tape! But that's not the end of it. In high school, I got my own CD-playing boombox for dance practice. Fast forward a few years and I purchased a MP3 player, and now I play music from my cell phone. Of course this is the abbreviated version, but in 40 years of my life, the way I listen to music has changed drastically. This timeline of change can also be said of my life. I am not the same little girl that had Smokey Robinson records ("Tears of a Clown" was my favorite song!) and no one expects me to be. But yet we get

> **We have to change because anything stagnant is dead. You have to be ready to navigate change - in your marriage, in yourself, and in your spouse.**

married hoping that our spouses never change or only change for the better - that's unrealistic. In *Becoming a Couple of Destiny*, Bishop Walker and Dr. Stephaine Walker write that "God creates a relationship for our 'not yet.' He knows how are lives are going to evolve, and strategically connects us to people who can handle where we are going."

Change is inevitable, yet humans don't like to change. Change is scary. It is also hard, uncertain, and often uncomfortable. Change can be positive as well. Change ushers in growth, increase, betterment. We have to change because anything stagnant is dead. You have to be ready to navigate change - in your marriage, in yourself, and in your spouse.

As the seasons of your life change, your spouse will, too. Ecclesiastes 3: 1-8 speaks of it this way:

> *There is a time for everything,*
>   *and a season for every activity under the heavens:*
> *2 a time to be born and a time to die,*
>   *a time to plant and a time to uproot,*
> *3 a time to kill and a time to heal,*
>   *a time to tear down and a time to build,*
> *4 a time to weep and a time to laugh,*
>   *a time to mourn and a time to dance,*
> *5 a time to scatter stones and a time to gather them,*
>   *a time to embrace and a time to refrain from embracing,*
> *6 a time to search and a time to give up,*
>   *a time to keep and a time to throw away,*
> *7 a time to tear and a time to mend,*
>   *a time to be silent and a time to speak,*
> *8 a time to love and a time to hate,*
>   *a time for war and a time for peace.*

There is a time and season for everything. In today's microwave society, we want everything now. Not in 20 seconds, not in 48 hours, not next week - we want it now. So the idea of riding the waves of change and being aware of the seasons is almost foreign to us. One example of this is any local gym the first warm spring day. It seems as if when the weather hits 80 degrees, everyone decides that it is time to get swimsuit ready. It's too late when it is 80 degrees outside. You have to hit the gym and put in work in the winter to be ready for swimsuit season. The way summer bodies are made in the winter is the same way you have to work hard in some seasons to reap the benefits in another.

Spouses have to know how to flourish in their current season while preparing for the next season. Every season isn't pretty. There will be some hard times and problem seasons. These are "valley" seasons. You have to do the work in the valley before you get to your next harvest. If you know how to navigate your seasons, you will be able to navigate marital change. In every season, ask yourself the following questions:

1. What is this season? Define the season. See it clearly for what it is.
2. What am I supposed to learn in this season? Every season teaches a lesson. What is this season teaching you about yourself, others, God?
3. What am I supposed to do in this season? Am I to start a business? Write a book? Have a baby?
4. What's on the horizon? Visualize your next season. What do you need to do now to prepare you for the next change?

By asking yourself these questions, you move from passive season dweller to focused season flourisher. If you manage your seasons well and understand their purpose, then you are more apt to understand your spouse's changes, too.

CONGRATS ON YOUR ENGAGEMENT: LETTERS TO TIFFANY

Heavy letter, huh? I know I threw a bunch of questions at you but your answers are so important to your journey. This wife thing is amazing but remember, it's a long term commitment! You'll want to go into it with clear expectations of who your lover-boy really is and who he is to become.

Be blessed, Sis!
Neysa

3

Dollars and Cents-ability

Come on, bride-to-be! Sing with me:

"Cause ain't nothin goin on but the rent/ You got to have a J-O-B if you wanna be with me."

If you are an 80s baby, you know this tune by Gwen Guthrie. For the younger folks, what about this classic Wu-tang joint:

"Cash rules everything around me/ CREAM get the money/ Dolla dolla bill y'all."

I bet you know that one, too. So why am I starting this letter with songs? I want to illustrate how money or lack thereof is so permeated throughout our culture, that songs about it are ingrained in our minds. Money is important to our lives and happiness. Therefore, money is important to your marriage. Some church folks believe that money is bad. But in 1

Timothy 6:10, the Bible reads "For the <u>love</u> of money is a root of all kinds of evil. Some people, eager for money, have wandered from the faith and pierced themselves with many griefs." Money isn't bad. Greed is bad. Using money for evil is bad. Money, however, is a neutral tool that transforms into an instrument of good or evil depending on who wields it.

Your ideas about money shape how you use it. The same holds true for your spouse. What's in his wallet is determined by his views on money. So how do you merge both of your ideas into one cohesive unit? Well, that's what we are going to tackle in this letter.

> **Your ideas about money - good or bad - shape how you use money. The same goes for your spouse. A successful marriage requires you to discuss those ideas and work together for your fiscal goals.**

Fiscal Transparency

So, what do you know about money? If you are like Chris and I, we knew nothing. When we got married, I knew we worked and we used the money to buy stuff. Tah-dah! It was that simple. Guess what happened when we had a credit card? Yep! We bought more stuff. Like so many people, we had a little money and even less fiscal knowledge. If you add those together, you get a mess! But do you want to know what was an even bigger mess? The fact that we didn't fix it. Not only did we not fix the problem, we didn't know *how* to fix the problem. We let debt climb and climb and climb and... well, you get the picture.

Congrats on Your Engagement: Letters to Tiffany

We knew our finances were a mess, and every so often, one of us would try to tackle the problem. After a short period of trying to fix our sad financial situation, we would get overwhelmed, give up, and bury our heads in the sand like little ostriches. If we were honest about it, the number one reason that we didn't buckle down and dig our way out was because we were embarrassed. We have college degrees. We are smart. We are the talented tenth. We should know how to fix it. But we didn't. We were broke and embarrassed about it. I bet we aren't the only ones. In fact in *The Total Money Makeover*, Dave Ramsey writes this about financial ignorance: "If you made a mess of your money and/or haven't gotten the best use from it, usually the reason is that you were never taught to do so. Ignorance doesn't mean dumb; it means you have to learn how." You have to learn to manage money. Instead of taking the time to seek out help, we wrongly believe we should just *know* how to use money and more importantly, make it work for us. Nothing could be further from the truth.

If you have financial wizards for parents or if you have parents that barely had two nickels to rub together, watching how they handle money has shaped your financial decisions. You either imitate their actions or you do the exact opposite. Parents either teach you what to do or what not to do, but either way, it's a lesson. Whatever your current financial status or history, you have to share it with your fiancé. I'm serious. You have to sit down with pen and paper and lay it all out. You have to tell each other exactly how much you have, who you owe, how much you owe, and how much you make. All of it. Every last cent. You can't hold anything back. You also have to talk about habits. You know that daily Starbucks habit that you have or that opening day of the new Jordans habit that he has? You have to share that as well.

Maybe you are a financial wunderkind and have saved every dime or maybe you have more Michael Kors purses than money, you have to tell him. You have to share it all - every penny - because financial secrets will poison a healthy marriage. Your future spouse has to know what you are good at and what your triggers are so together you can successfully navigate the next 50 years.

This is hard. No one wants to admit to making poor financial decisions. It makes us feel ashamed and ignorant. We have to change the way we look at transparency and fiscal openness. Transparency gives your beloved a chance to see all of you - flaws and all. This openness also gives you a chance to start working as a team to build a future. Most folks feel they can handle any problem if they know up front about the problem. Personally, I hate not knowing about a fiscal problem. When I have advance knowledge of a bill or a debt, I can change my spending habits to help correct the mistake. Let's say your spouse spent too much money on a new video game system, but you receive an unexpected medical bill. If you don't know about the money spent on the game and the medical bill, you may not know that you shouldn't buy that new Coach bag. In fact you could buy the bag and make the financial problem worse. If your spouse tells you in advance about any financial deficits, you can delay the purchase until a more appropriate time.

Reflection

Whatcha got, Boo? Look, put down the money shame. Money management is NOT my area of expertise. I am sure my fiscal planner is laughing at me writing this chapter. But this isn't 401k or retirement advice. This is *marriage* advice. And the first step of getting your money together is really facing your financial situation. So back to my original question—whatcha got, Boo?

1. How much money do you have in your accounts right now? If you went to the bank and withdrew all your money, are you walking out with a bag of money or some change?
2. How much debt do you owe - both good and bad debt? The store credit cards, the student loans, the mortgage, the $20 you owe your cousin...list it all.
3. What do you make from all your streams of income? Your 9 to 5, your MaryKay business, your Etsy store...you earned it, so list it.
4. What lessons did your parents teach you about money and money management?
5. Finally, how does money and conversations about money make you feel?

All these things make up your personal financial picture. That last question is key to your financial freedom and your transparency. If you feel money shame, then you may be inclined to hide money or debt from your love. Don't. Acknowledging the emotions tied to your money management allows you to change the narrative. You may have had money shame but you are moving towards money success.

Neysa E. Taylor

Yours, Mine, Ours

For years you have been handling - or mishandling - your own finances. Your spouse has been doing the same. Now that you've decided to be a married unit, all of that financial individuality is out the window, right? Well, yes and no. While it's true that you are about to be a cohesive unit, you do get to retain some individuality. We all need this. We all need some autonomy in our lives. Before you can access this freedom, you have to first put in work cleaning up your own mess.

You don't want to saddle your future hubs with your money mistakes. In the book, *Girl, Get Your Money Straight*, Glinda Bridgforth recommends checking your net worth and the motivation for your financial habits. Look at the receipts in your purse. Do you spend more when you are depressed? Are you a habitual shopper? Are you a secret online shopper? Is Amazon Prime your boo? You have to uncover your habits so you can tackle your debt. If you address your debt without addressing your habits, you will be back in the same pattern of misspending. (Trust me on this one!)

There is a way to have a joint portfolio and keep some individuality. In an interview with ABC News, comedian/talk show host/radio announcer Steve Harvey explained it this way:

Every couple should have four bank accounts: two individual spending money accounts and two joint accounts for essential spending and saving. The savings account should require two signatures to move the money."

Ohh, yeah! That is a plan that I can get behind. Of course, you will have to converse with your spouse and determine what percentage you will put in your personal spending accounts. Most couples don't make the exact same amount of money so you have to determine what amount is appropriate to put aside in your personal spending accounts. This system gives you a bit a freedom to make your own purchases without oversight. This individual account comes in handy when you want to surprise your spouse with a gift or a vacation or maybe that Coach bag I mentioned earlier. But for any of this to work, you must communicate.

Reflection

Were you excited about having a bit of financial freedom in the midst of a marriage? Yeah, me too! But don't just ball out on your money then go to your fiance for a loan midway through the month. That's not fair to him and undermines the financial freedom you desire.

Do you ever wonder where your money goes? Yep, me too. Try this really low brow exercise. Put a sandwich baggie in your purse. For one week, put the receipts from everything you purchase in the bag. Every. Single. Thing. Gum, Starbucks, lunch…all of it. At the end of the week, pull them out and analyze them. Are you spending too much in some areas? This is a self check so you can make corrections and have money to take your love out on a surprise date later in the month.

Neysa E. Taylor

Using Business Solutions to Mind Your Personal Business

Think about your career. How do you know what you are supposed to do each day, each quarter, each year? I assume that when you started your career, you went through an orientation. This is true for any position. No one hires an individual and says, "Welcome to the company - good luck! See you later." If they do, I am sure they won't be in business very long. Now that you are fully in your position, you have frequent staff meetings and attend trainings to keep your skills fresh. Good companies invest in their employees at the start of their careers and throughout their employment. This is doubly true for your marriage and your marriage finances. So many people manage multi-million dollar accounts at work but don't use the same principles to manage their marriage and personal accounts. So let's take a look at how business knowledge can help your union.

Orientation

When you get a new position, one of the first things your supervisor does is explain the job duties and what is expected of you. Have you ever asked your fiancé to define the wife position for you? Do you know what he expects? Do you know if he believes that his wife will meet him at the door with a cognac and his slippers? Does he expect you to be barefoot and pregnant? Does he believe that household chores should be shared? Have you told him what you expect out of a husband? Do you expect to stay home and quit your career? You both have to define the positions so that your future spouse can know exactly what you expect.

This will help you determine if you can - or even want to - meet his expectations. Talking with your fiancé about the position allows him to make choices as well.

Also, what are your goals as a family? Any good corporation has goals and key performance indicators that tell you if you are achieving those goals. A company has to have a clear direction for it to grow and make progress. Do you want to own a business, purchase real estate, or travel the world? Do you want to retire at 45? Include your financial goals when developing your united vision. Define your future and set corporate goals to achieve this future. These are milestones that keep you moving in the right direction.

Staff Meetings

I am blessed to have the best staff in the world, and while I don't micromanage them, I do believe in frequently checking in to keep us focused. Every Monday at 9 a.m., I call my staff together to discuss our goals and plan for the week. While common goals are laid out at the beginning of the fiscal year, these weekly meetings help everyone stay on task. Another benefit of the weekly meeting is that if a member of the team is having difficulty with a project, they can ask for help at that time. You need this type of meeting for your family as well. Once you have a vision of where you are going, you have to check in periodically to ensure you are both walking in the same direction.

Now, those that know me know that I can be a bit nerdy. When our family started having family meetings, it felt awkward. So awkward that we quit having them. But then I realized my approach was wrong. I had a typed agenda and weekly schedule. I wanted to solve the problems of the family in one meeting. I also ran the meeting like my family was my staff. That was a huge problem! No one wants to sit in a meeting for hours. You don't want to do it at work, much less at home. The family meeting should be led by the husband but have a "roundtable" feel. Also, when you have children, I suggest having two meetings: 10 minutes of just you and your husband and 10 minutes for the entire family. Your children should not be privy to everything that is happening in your household but need to see how a well-managed family is run. You can't shelter them from everything. They have to learn how to manage both good and bad times. They also need to see that they play a part in setting the goals and obtaining the goals for the family. Our meeting agenda looks like this:

Parent Meeting:

I. Money update - How much do you have right now?
II. Bills - What's been paid? What needs to be paid?
III. Debt - Who do we owe? How are we doing on paying down debt?
IV. You Good? - This is the check in with your love to see if ya'll are thriving as a unit. Any issues you need to discuss across a table before the kids walk in. (Note: this is not the time to start an argument. The kids are joining you in 10 minutes and you don't want them walking into a tense kitchen.)
V. New Business

Family Meeting:

I. Money update - What do you have? What do you need this week?

II. What events do you have this week?
III. Grades and Homework
IV. New Business/Discussion
V. Prayer

This agenda keeps us on track as a cohesive unit and ensures that we are moving forward together. Guess, what? This is my agenda. You can use it, remix it like Diddy, or write your own from scratch. Together you determine how to best run your meetings.

Continuing Education

Another practice we can learn from the corporate world is investing in continuing education. When I think about continuing education, I have to think about my career. My supervisor hired me because my skill set matched the current needs of the company and the industry. But we all know that companies and industries change. I have to invest in continuing education to ensure that my skills stay sharp. You can't rest on your laurels. You have to always learn more and push forward to stay relevant in your career.

Your family is the same way. You have to do continuing education for your marriage. Read books on marriage (you are off to a great start). Attend workshops, conferences and retreats. Go to marriage counseling before you need marriage counseling. Take financial planning classes to help you achieve your dreams. Invest in your union. You want this marriage to last for 80+ years, so protect your investment of time, love and purpose but continuously improving.

Friend, as you are planning for your wedding, I bet you've studied invitations, bridal gown designers, and scoured reception venues. You have invested in learning all about weddings so you can get it perfect for your big day. Also, remember you've spent years investing in other education too. Between formal education and the time spent at work, you have gathered a great deal of information on leadership, teamwork, emotional intelligence, and more. Employing business principles to help your marriage is a wise use of all of that knowledge you've amassed. There's no job more important than the one you are about to embark upon. There is no team more important than #TeamMarriage.

You've got this, Love!
Neysa

4

Praise and Worship

My joyful bride-to-be,

I know you're probably thinking about your wedding, the white dress, the ornate cake, and the tuxedos. Most people do when they think about marriage.

Some (maybe you?) may even think about white picket fences and chubby babies. All of that has a place, but when you think about marriage - not a *wedding* but a marriage - I want you to think about two gray-haired people in a hospital room. One lies dying in a hospital bed hooked to machines that beep constantly and give painkillers to provide a bit of comfort. The other sits in a chair by their side in prayer. That is really the image of marriage that we should all strive to achieve. I call this the "Simon love." As Jesus was being led to His death, He became too weak to carry His cross. Simon was forced to carry it to Calvary. Simon's strength was needed so that Jesus could fulfill His Father's mission. At some point in your marriage, your strength is going to fail. I know you think you are strong, but if Jesus ran out of strength, and He is JESUS, then your strength will surely fail you, too. Is your fiancé the man who will pick up the cross and carry it for you? Will he pray for you and with you as you take your final breath? Are you the type of woman who can cover your husband when he falters? Will you be able to stand watch over him as he prepares to die?

That's a heavy thing to consider. Can you stand watch over someone as they take their last breath? If the answer is no, then call the engagement off right now. You aren't ready to be married. Seriously. Don't think you have 60+ years to get it together. People get terminal diseases or have fatal accidents at any age. That may sound depressing and morbid, but you have to be ready to cover your spouse in their moment of need. In 2012, Christopher was diagnosed with colon cancer. By August of that year, he was so sick that I thought he would die. I was scared. He wasn't forty yet. Praise God that he made it through, but it goes to show that illness and sometimes death are always around the bend. You have to be ready or as the senior saints say "don't be found wanting."

In the first letter, I wrote about how engagement is a time of preparation. This preparation is on all fronts but most importantly the spiritual one. You want to choose a partner that you can be equally yoked with for life. While salvation is an individual relationship with God, your journey is a shared one. The only way you can grow

> **While salvation is an individual relationship with God, your journey is a shared one.**

together spiritually is to make praise a part of you. Now let's explore each one in depth.

Equally Yoked

Equally yoked. Singles ministries around the globe talk about finding a partner who is "equally yoked," but what does it mean? Let me tell you what it doesn't mean first. Have you ever been sitting around drinking a latte with your sista circle talking about men and how hard it is to find a man? In that conversation did anyone mention being equally yoked? Did your girlfriends give a list of attributes that they are looking for to make them equally yoked? Like a luxury car, two degrees, a job making $60-thousand a year, buns of steel, abs for days, and teeth so white that Colgate would be jealous. Not to mention the other attributes that they want. They want someone able to talk politics, dance, play b-ball in the hood, wear a tuxedo and some Timberlands. Your friends say they deserve a man like this because they have most of those attributes, too. I bet you are nodding right now. Well, hold up. That isn't equally yoked. That is a wish list.

The Word says, "Do not be yoked together with unbelievers. For what do righteousness and wickedness have in common? Or what fellowship can light have with darkness?" (2 Corinthians 6:14) I believe that you have to be on the same page to move forward in the covenant of marriage. I know many people are married to people of different religions or non-believers, and it works for them. That's great for them. But for a covenant marriage, you will need JESUS to make it through.

In *Love and Intimacy: Five Ways to Get Together and Stay Together,* Bishop Joseph W. Walker III writes:

> We have to remember that marriage is a covenant between two people and God. Scripture is specific about this because with God covenant-making was

essential and unequivocal - so much so that God demonstrated it by the price of shared blood. Covenant always involved sacrifice. Jesus Christ obviously demonstrated this on the cross. We forget that it takes blood, sweat, and tears to make covenant happen. Wherever there's covenant, somebody's got to bleed for it.

When Chris and I were first married, we weren't in relationship with Christ. We attended church on a regular basis but didn't have a *personal relationship* with Jesus. Through our trials and tribulations, I moved from being a pew sitter to a Jesus chaser. I want Him to be proud of me. I want all of the blessings and promises He has for my life to come to pass. I still make tons of mistakes but I want to live right. As I was developing a relationship with Christ, guess who wasn't? Yep, Chris. So while I was praying and believing, Chris was just stumbling. Well, let's just say that prayer wasn't on the top of his things to do list. We were <u>not</u> equally yoked.

Praise God that Chris now has a relationship with Jesus, too. He had to get to a place of surrender like I did. He had to want to change and when he did, it was marvelous. But don't be like us, be better than us. You want to be in a relationship where you both believe in God.

Make Praise a Part of You

It takes anywhere from 21-30 days to create a habit. At least that's what everyone says. Whether it's 21 days or 60 days, it all starts with day one. You have to create a spiritual practice that you can sustain. Do you go to church on Sunday? Bible Study? What about morning or evening prayer? Is praise and worship part of your daily habit? I know that when I am focused and life isn't crazy, I am really intentional about spending time with the Lord. You can call it coincidence, karma, or just bad timing, but when I am not intentional about my time with God, my life spirals out of control. It is a vicious cycle. I get too busy for one day and my whole attitude changes. Before I know it, I am busier and busier and honestly, forget to make time for God. How stupid does that sound? I forget to make time for God. God. THE God. But it happens. And normally my life goes so far off the rails that I get a supernatural knock upside the head that forces me to reconsider my lifestyle and practices. At that moment I start thinking, "Aha, I hear you, God. I'm back."

Reflection

Personal prayer time is fundamental. Do you have a meditation/prayer schedule? Let's delve into that a bit deeper.

1. What do you believe?
2. Do you know what your beloved believes?
3. How much time do you spend in prayer and meditation each day or week?
4. Do you feel like or desire to spend more time with God?

5. Do you actively participate in a community of believers (church, temple, mosque, etc.)?

I did not have any of these things in place when I got married. Don't be me. Be better than me. Heck, that is why I am writing this for you. Make your time with God part of your DAILY schedule. I am not going to define it for you. I am not going to tell you to take 15 minutes in the morning or go into your war room at night. I am going to tell you to do it. There are morning devotionals. There's *Fervent* by Priscilla Shirer. Or check out *Greater* by Steven Furtick. There are tons of tomes and apps that can help you organize your prayer life. Set a reminder in your schedule and make the time a priority. You have to do it. Your spouse has to do it. And then you have to find time to do it together.

A Shared Individual Journey

When you die and get to the pearly gates, you will have to answer for your life, your actions, your belief. There's no Southwest Airlines buddy pass into heaven. You have to answer for your life. Your spouse will have to answer for his. You can pray for each other, and you can pray together, but at the end of the day, your relationship with God is personal. Do you firmly understand that fact? I hope so because what I am going to say next may make you say, "What a minute. You just said...." Here goes: while your relationship with God is personal, it can influence your spouse both positively and negatively. Think about a friend who is trying to live healthily. If you go eat lunch together every day, and she is eating salads and grilled chicken, and you are eating burgers and fries, one of you will eventually slide over to the habits of the other. Maybe you will start ordering fruit cups instead of fries, or maybe she will start getting less fit choices. Either way, you will influence each other. This is true for your spiritual life as well.

You and your spouse may not be on the same chapter spiritually. That's ok. But every step you take toward God will bring the two of you closer together. That is a win-win. Look at this graphic:

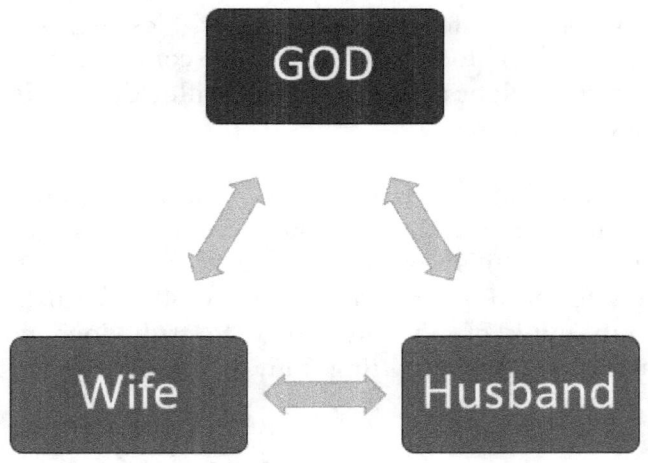

You and your spouse are individuals. You have individual journeys, but as you walk along your path and grow closer to Jesus, you and your spouse will draw closer as well. Isn't that an amazing thing?! Let's be real - drawing closer to God is a big enough "prize," but He sweetens the pot by making a relationship with Him benefit your marriage as well.

Your personal prayer time can benefit your spouse in other ways as well. In *The Power of a Praying Wife,* author Stormie Omartian shares the benefit of covering your husband (or fiance') in prayer. She writes:

The power of a praying wife is not a means of gaining control over your husband, so don't get your hopes up! In fact, it is quite the opposite. It's laying down all claim to power in and of yourself, and relying on God's power to transform you, your husband, your circumstances, and your marriage.

She later adds "It's a way to invite God's power into your husband's life for his greatest blessing, which is ultimately yours, too." If that doesn't convince you to fall on your knees right now, maybe this will… the words of her husband. He shares

> I cannot imagine what my life would be without her praying for me. It gives me comfort and security, and also fulfills the mission the Lord has for us to pray for each other and bear one another's burdens. I can think of no better way to truly love your husband than by lifting him up in prayer on a consistent basis.

So are you on your knees now? I thought so. Let me tell you what NOT to do. Don't see an issue and pray for your man, then two days later look at God with an attitude like "I know you heard me. When are you gon' fix that?" It does not work that way. Don't mistake God for the genie on Aladdin. He doesn't grant wishes. He makes promises. He gives blessings, favor, and mercy. He also corrects when necessary.

Let me tell you a story. When Chris and I were feuding, I thought "let me try prayer." I wish I could say that it was out of a deep spiritual movement but it wasn't. I was just tired and had tried everything else. So I prayed. While I was praying I was peeping at Chris looking for any sign of change. Guess what? Nothing changed. You can't be truly in God's presence and side eyeing the next person. It doesn't work like that. I had to close both of my eyes, focus on God and really pray. While I was praying, God changed me and later changed him.

I still pray for Chris. Sometimes it's a long conversation, other times it's a simple "Bless him, Lord." But I cover my husband. You should do the same.

Hey, Sis, you need faith. You do. I cannot stress the importance of a prayer life enough. Honestly, don't be hard headed like me. If your prayer life is not where it needs to be, dig deep right now. Not patty-cake, "Now I lay me down to sleep" prayer life either. You need some spiritual armor (to protect you), food (to sustain you) and weaponry (to fight back).

Be blessed!
Neysa

5

Learning to Survive the Storms

Sis,

I hope these letters are helping you so far. So you're preparing yourself for marriage and you love your fiancé just as he is. The two of you go to church every Sunday and Wednesday, so the faith piece is on lock. You might now be thinking that everything will be fine now, right?

Well, er...no.

Matthew 5:45 states "the rain falls on the just and unjust." That line means that no matter what, storms will come to pass. When I first read that verse, I hated it. Why live righteously when bad things happen to good people just like they do bad ones? Later I came to understand that while storms come to pass, having Jesus gives you the strength to handle the rain, the ability to overcome the wind, and the power to say "peace be still" in the midst of the turbulence.

Let me tell you, storms will come. Not just little stay inside thunderstorms, but raging blow your house down, I don't know which way is up, Dorothy-You're-Not-In-Kansas-Anymore storms. These storms *will* hurt and shake you to your core. You may be thinking, "No, we're in love. We don't have storms." But notice I said *will* hurt you and shake you, not *may* hurt you. The storms will come. Matter of fact, let me name a few for you: unemployment, recession, sickness, death in the family, infertility, injury, miscarriage, cancer, depression, etc. I'm sorry to tell you that at least one, but probably more, of these storms will attack you. Having a strong covenant marriage will allow you to not only endure life's hardships but survive the storms.

I really believed that all of our storms had passed before we got married. We'd endured some really significant storms before we said "I do." We broke up, got back together, had a kid (Hey, AT!), broke up "permanently" for a few years, dated other folks, and then realized that we were meant to be together. You do know that this is the abbreviated version, right? The made for tv version when in reality those years were jacked up and full of tears; full of "I miss him/I hate him/but I love him" moments. After we reconciled and I stood at the altar, I was so happy. I seriously thought, "God, thank you. You've brought us through the fire, and now we are on to our best life ever." I really believed that. In my novice faith, I thought that you went through a trial—singular, just one trial—and that was it. Voila! Now on to your best life ever. Well, I have since learned that we are stupid, and satan is patient. Every problem we face is not at the hands of the enemy. Quite often, we create problems with our own stupidity. Our lack of knowledge and preparation comes back to bite us all of the time. Other times, storms are created by the enemy to throw us off our path. John 10:10 states, "The thief comes only to steal and kill and destroy." His whole purpose, his only job is to make your life hell so that you can end up there. And Satan never misses a day of work. That's why you have to be prepared.

Carry an Umbrella

Every morning I wake up and turn on NewsChannel 5 in Nashville, Tennessee. While I used to work there and love listening to the news, the real reason I turn to NewsChannel5 is for Lelan Statom—the chief meteorologist. I know that every few minutes, Lelan will give me a weather update. This information is critical to my day. Is it going to be windy? Do I put on a jacket? How's the humidity? Do I flat iron my hair? Is it super-hot? Do I need to wear a dark suit to work? Is it getting chilly outside? Do I need to put on layers? Is it going to rain today? Do I need to carry an umbrella? It may not be raining right now, but do I need to pack an umbrella just in case?

The same is true for your prayer life. You should have a spiritual "umbrella" with you at all times. Remember what I said, storms *will* come. Storms. Plural tense. So if you know that, why aren't you always prepared for them?

Being prepared means deliberately spending time with God every day. Prayer. Meditation. Reading the Bible. Worship. Gathering with other believers.

> **Prayer is your spiritual umbrella. Being prepared is spending time with God every day.**

All of these things build up your spiritual reserves. You need a spiritual emergency fund or emergency backpack.

Think about this. The Federal Emergency Management Agency (FEMA) has a list of things you can do to be prepared for a national emergency. They recommend things like having water, a meeting place for family, a flashlight, and other essential items. Most financial advisors suggest having a 3 - 6 month financial emergency fund. This money should be easily accessible and is designed to carry you through a financial drought. The same mindset needs to be applied to your spiritual life as well. You need a reservoir of faith to carry you through the hard times.

There is a scripture for every need you may have. The Bible is full of triumphant stories and motivation to get us through trials. Too often, we don't open the book and ask for help.

Worried? Scared? Look no further than Psalm 23. Pay special attention to verse 4: "Even though I walk through the darkest valley, I will fear no evil, for You are with me; Your rod and Your staff, they comfort me."

Feeling overwhelmed? Try Psalm 91: 14-16:

14 "Because he[a] loves me," says the Lord, "I will rescue him;
I will protect him, for he acknowledges my name.
15 He will call on me, and I will answer him;
I will be with him in trouble,
I will deliver him and honor him.
16 With long life I will satisfy him
and show him my salvation."

Anything you need, you can find there. Don't worry if you aren't a Bible scholar. This is an instance where Google is your friend. But the more you turn to the Bible, the more equipped you will be to withstand the storms of life.

I can tell you that I have struggled with this myself. The truth is we all do. Every. Single. Person. Don't let anyone tell you differently. There are days when your faith is on fire, and you are immersed in the Word. You are focused and praying and ready for any problem that comes your way. There are also days when you are struggling. Trust me when I say that those are the days when you have to dig in deep even more. Here's why: earlier this year I was frustrated, fed up, and tired. I was spent. So I decided that I was going to forgo my morning prayer and meditation. Now, my morning prayer time is really eclectic. It could be a prayer, devotional reading, playing gospel music, or a bit of meditation. But I was tired and frustrated and I thought, "Eh, just skip it this morning." Nine months later, I came to my senses and realized just how far off the path I had gotten.

But the good news is that God doesn't move. Let me say it again. God. Doesn't. Move. When I finally opened my eyes, I realized there is a part b to the Bible verse I mentioned earlier (John 10:10). The Word says that "I have come that they may have life, and have it to the fullest." That line is what gives me hope even when I have to jump start my own faith.

Neysa E. Taylor

<u>Reflection</u>

Do you have a spiritual umbrella? If not, let's start putting a spiritual emergency kit together.
1. Think about your life thus far. What do you read or listen to when you need to recenter?
2. Do you have a place that aligns your spirit?
3. Are there quotes or scripture that lift your spirit?

Write these things down in a journal that you keep close by. You have to know where your emergency kit is located at all times. Imagine your kitchen catching fire. You can't spend time running around looking for your fire extinguisher. You have to know where it is located because time is of the essence. Or think about it this way, if you come home to find your house has been robbed, you don't start calling around to police precincts to ask for help. You know that if you call 911, help will come. Your faith in 911 is so great that you teach it to your kids at an early age. Every kindergartener knows to call 911 for the police. The same should be true for your spiritual 911 kit. In a crisis, you don't have time to go searching for an answer. You need to be prepared.

Attack the Problem, Not Each Other

Imagine your family on a boat adrift at sea. In the middle of the night, you realize that your boat is taking on water. So what do you do? Do you fuss

> Your spouse is your ultimate teammate. When problems arise - no matter how big or how small - you are supposed to tackle them together.

about whose bright idea it was to take a cruise, or do you all start bailing water? Most folks would say, "Well, that's a no brainer. I would grab the nearest bucket and start bailing water." But in all honesty, many people would actually start arguing and pointing fingers at each other.

Your spouse is your ultimate teammate. When problems arise—no matter how big or how small—you are supposed to tackle them together. When there is a problem on the horizon, you have to stay focused on attacking the problem, not each other. That sounds easy enough. Trust me. It's not. Well, maybe it is for you, but for me it was (is) a struggle. Let me tell you a bit about my personality. I am an offensive player. If there is trouble on the horizon, I am ready to run at it and attack it before it comes to my door. My handsome husband is a defensive player. If he sees trouble coming, he prefers to wait and see if it comes to our doorstep before acting. We approach trouble fundamentally different, and those differences caused a lot of strife in our relationship. I would point out danger on the horizon, and when he didn't act or respond the way I believed he should, then I was angry. Really angry. I couldn't understand why he didn't follow my instructions so that the problem would never get to our front door. But I had to realize that sometimes my husband has to deal with his problems his way. I can't stunt his growth or belittle his approach by always expecting him to handle things my way. Do you know how frustrating that is?!

He was equally frustrated with me and my offensive approach. Instead of wait and see, I at times run into battle without a fully thought out plan of attack. You can probably guess that at times my approach actually made whatever problem we were facing worse. So we were arguing with each other, and the problem is just sitting there winning. We had to learn to go with the ebb and flow of the situation, to really dig in deep and support whoever was taking the lead in addressing the problem. Attacking each other just wastes energy, and you need all of your energy to attack the problem.

In horror movies, I never understood why people don't work together to fight the bad guy. The evil monster/ghost/zombie/killer is outside the room, and the folks in the room are arguing about what got them in the situation. Why aren't they assessing their surroundings, sharing knowledge, and figuring out how to fight together? To avoid being attacked by the evil, monstrous problem, like the victims of a horror movie, we have to focus on fighting the problems *with* our spouse, not fighting our spouse *with* our problems.

September 11, 2001 was a scary day. The attack on the United States shook the entire nation to its core, but there was one element of good that came out of that day. That day, everyone in the United States - no matter their race, creed, or status - was *American*. We were in this together. The Pledge of Allegiance is something school children across this country recite daily. But on 9/11, we were really "One Nation" and "Indivisible." That's how your marriage should be. While it shouldn't take a tragedy to make you appreciate each other, you should unify in times of struggle and strife. One marriage under God... Indivisible.

Reflection

I bet you didn't just meet your fiance' yesterday. You've probably bumped heads a time or two in the past. Think about your last fight:

1. What did you notice about your "fighting" styles?
2. Do you stick to your corners and have trouble compromising?

3. Does one of you yell while the other retreats and gives the silent treatment?
4. How did you resolve the issue?

Understanding how each of you de-escalates a disagreement can help you in the future. If I know that Chris only yells when he is super angry, I know what triggers to avoid. Likewise, Chris knows that my voice lowers and I start my "courtroom cross examination" voice when I am peeved beyond control. Like in poker, knowing the "tells" of each person helps us keep the conversation in the compromise zone instead of the combat zone.

Dance in the Rain

"I'm singing in the rain, just singing in the rain…"

You've heard that song before. If you are like me, you picture a small giggling child in a yellow raincoat and rainboots, jumping in puddles. That vision epitomizes the act of turning a bad situation into a blessing. While no one is grateful for storms, if you focus on the blessings you can dance in the rain.

We've already talked about drawing on your spiritual reserves and not attacking each other. Dancing in the rain takes it one step further. You have to build up your partner. You have to focus on each other. You can give each other wise counsel. Spouses must stand together in battle, pray over and support each other. You have to pick your fiancé up when they get knocked down. You have to become their safe place in the storm.

In the Northeastern part of the U.S., beautiful lighthouses adorn the coasts. These tall structures with bright lights atop them are not there for decoration. These buildings help provide navigation to the ships at sea. I'm no sailor, but even I know that on clear nights, the lighthouse really isn't needed. The captain can navigate the water by stars or the light of the moon. Lighthouses are even more important when the ships are in stormy waters or cloudy, moonless nights. The light emanating from the lighthouse beckons the ships to safe harbors. It signals that if you make it to the source of this light, then you are ok. You are safe. You have to be that safe harbor for your husband, and he needs to be the same for you. Your favorite place to be, to recharge, to rest should be in the arms of your spouse. When you know that your spouse is the earthly manifestation of Godly love, then God's agape love flows through your spouse to you to recharge your batteries when you are running dry.

Notice when your spouse is tired, frustrated, or just beaten. Love on him a bit more. Listen a bit more. Compliment him a bit more. When his armor is battered and bruised, your actions and kind words are what welds out the dents and shines his shield so that he is ready to face battle again the next day. You can't battle on two fronts. It's impossible. You need a place to recharge, and the arms of your love should be that place.

I love going to the movies. In many romantic comedies or "chick flicks," you see characters get depressed and then go on a long sabbatical. During this break, the character gets time to think things over and start life again. While I am not saying that a fresh start is not possible, more often than not, you will have to deal with your situations without a trip around the world. But you can find moments of happiness. Even on days where life is hard, find a moment of "it's just me and you, and we are ok." Grab a bottle of wine and picnic in the yard. Take $2 and get a McDonald's sundae and eat it at the park. Rent a movie from the library and make it a free "Netflix and chill" night. Hold hands. Do something - anything - together. Show the enemy and each other that no matter how hard it gets, you are facing life's challenges together.

<u>Reflection</u>

Let's make a list of those *just you and me* moments.

1. What are those things that you love to do together? Where are the places you love to go?
2. What type of dates did you go on early in your dating life with your love?
3. Are there places you haven't been but want to visit together?
4. Revisit all of the lists you just made. Are they all from your viewpoint of are there things that your fiance' likes to do too? If not, make a "this isn't really my thing but I love this man" list.

Sis, this man is your teammate. You said "yes" to the ring and have decided to make this team your home. It is up to the two of you to protect it, defend it and nurture it. The only way to keep your marriage safe is to work together both on the sunny days and during the thunderstorms.

Keep shining, girl!
Neysa

6

Circle of Friends

My dear bride-to-be,

There is an African proverb that goes "If you want to go fast, go alone. But if you want to go far, go with others." Well, Pinterest said it was an African proverb, and I like it, so let's go with it. No woman or man is an island unto themselves. You probably have a posse, a squad, a sister circle, friends, coworkers, sorority sisters, and church folks. If you are alive and not a hermit, you should have a team, and your hubs hopefully has one, too. If you add in social media "friends," your clique can be far reaching.

In this world of friends and followers, how do you know who your confidantes are? Who are the people you can trust with information about your mate and your marriage? Some people will advise that you never talk about your marriage to anyone. They say your marriage is just for you and your spouse, and everyone else should remain outside that circle. There are benefits to that way of thinking. Your marriage is sacred and should be protected. But while I agree with the sanctity of marriage, I also believe that many people need a safe place to vent also. If you are nodding and saying, "Exactly," please hold up a minute. Let me tell you what happens when you vent in unsafe places. I know someone who I will call Teysa Naylor. Teysa found out that her husband was having an affair and was so upset that she posted it on a social media site as her status. Yes. She. Did. It was Facebook to be exact. Mind you, this was back when Facebook was still in its early stages, and social media rules were still being formed. But not only did she post it, she posted it and took a nap. Now, when I—I mean, she—woke up from that nap, she had a gazillion instant messages and text messages.

You may be wondering why would anyone do that? I heard that Teysa was just tired, fed up, and broken. She said that she wanted to post it so that she would no longer have to put on a strong face when she felt like she was dying. She posted it to inflict harm on her spouse by embarrassing him, and discrediting his "good guy" image. She posted it to close the door on her marriage because who could reconcile after all of that? While I understand all of Teysa's reasoning, it was wrong. Posting pain on a social media site is just inviting an audience into your life. It may feel like you are getting support but really you are just turning your marriage into a bad reality TV show.

While social media is the wrong place to talk about your union, you can talk about your marriage in a safe place. Do you know how to determine who is safe and who isn't? Let's start with doing a friendship assessment. Look at the people whom you call friends. Eighty percent (80%) of the folks that you call friends are really acquaintances. These are the peripheral, happy hour folks. Another ten percent (10%) are house party friends. You know folks that you would actually allow inside your home if you had a house party.

They get the privilege of knowing your address and sitting on your couch. Eight percent (8%) are really friends. These friends come to your birthday party with gifts and show up at a relative's funeral with a pound cake. Just two percent (2%) are confidantes. These are ride or die, prayer warriors, love you in spite of yourself friends. These are the folks that will let you cry on their floor or drive you to the hospital and stay with you. Do you see the difference?

Reflection

Look at your circle and do a team assessment.

1. Can you discern which friends fall into the different categories?
2. Have you ever mistrusted a friend? How did you feel when they betrayed that confidence? Was it a mistake or malicious?
3. Who are your confidantes?

Take the time to think about categorizing your supporting cast. Only then will you know who is really your wise counsel.

Seek Wise Counsel

Let me tell you about my BFF, or as the tweens say "best friend forever." My best friend in the entire world is Keri Kelly. (She is going to kill me for putting her real, government name in this letter, but there isn't another name that will do my Keri - so very - justice.) God truly blessed me when we crossed paths at Tennessee State University many, many moons ago. Keri is the anti-Neysa. Where I am impulsive, she is thoughtful. Where I am emotional, she is rational. There are many times where I've called her and immediately she will cut through the B.S. and ask, "So, what's really going on?" While those qualities make Keri a great friend, the real reason she is my best friend is that she *never* judges. Ever. If I am wrong, she'll point that out, but she never puts me on the gallows or holds a grudge. Whenever something is amiss, she will immediately put me or my family on her personal prayer list. She is the epitome of a BFF. Keri is the "Chief Justice" of my wise counsel. She is so good at being a BFF that at her wedding shower, no less than six people stood up and talked about how Keri - my KERI - was their best friend! What?! And I can't even be mad because she personifies the kind of amazingness that everyone wants in their lives.

So who is your Keri? Not five Keris, but *a* Keri. See Keris are special and rare. Everyone that you have as a friend, even some you might consider best friend level, is not privy to your marriage. Marriage is a marathon not a sprint. Have you ever had a friend with that awful boyfriend, and they would break up, then make up, then break up again? Yep. Well, in marriage there may be days—many days—when you'll want to throw in the towel. A great friend will let you vent, but will not hold it against you when you invite her to dinner with you and your boo the next week. She won't give you the side-eye. Instead she will pray for your marriage and ask God to give you the answer. Do you have a Keri? I hope so, but if you don't, take a look at yourself. Are you a "Keri" for anyone? It is hard to find a confidante if no one can confide in you.

Reflection

What type of friend are you? Seriously, you can't look at your circle without looking at yourself first.

1. Are you a good friend to others?
2. Do you judge your friends for decisions they make that differ from your opinion?
3. Do you pray for your friends?

You have to *be* a good friend to *have* good friends. If you can't find true friends in your friend assessment, then you probably need to do some soul searching. If you are gossipy and messy, then you may need to change your ways and clean up your circle before you can find a person you can trust with your marriage.

Judas was a Friend of Jesus

In the age of social media, people seem to have an abundance of friends. Notice that I said "seem." Old folks used to say that every friendly face isn't your friend. Or in the words of Lauryn Hill:

> Beware the false motives of others
> Be careful of those who pretend to be brothers
> And you never suppose it's those who are closest to you
> To you
> They say all the right things, to gain their position
> Then use your kindness as their ammunition
> To shoot you down in the name of ambition, they do
> *(lyrics from "Forgive Them Father")*

We've all experienced a friend hurt. You know when a friend does something that really cuts you and hurts your feelings or spirit. Sometimes, these are arguments, and you get over it. Other times, friendships are ended because of the malfeasance. Either way, it hurts.

Sometimes, there is a Judas in your camp. We all know how Judas betrayed Jesus, so don't think that you are immune from having a Judas in your camp as well. A Judas is different than a regular friend that hurts your feelings. A Judas hurts you out of personal gain. That's the difference. A Judas tells your secrets to gain favor with another group. A Judas can be invited into your home and try to walk out with your husband. A Judas is scandalous and only out for her/himself.

This is why you must use discernment when you categorize your circle. You must ask God to show you where folks should be placed on the friendship hierarchy. Do the same for his friends. If you see Judas-like behavior in his friends, bring it to his attention. Protect your hubs from Judases, too.

Veto Power

This is a hard subject to talk about, but hear me out before passing judgment. I believe that you and your spouse should have the power to veto one another's friends. And by veto I really mean the power to ban your spouse from seeing another person.

Go ahead. Hiss. Grimace. Think, "What! She is trippin'. He can't tell me who I can and can't hang out with." Well, wait a minute. I am not saying that you should veto Vinny because he belches loud after he drinks beer, and you think that is nasty. (It is by the way). Nope, I am not saying that. What I am saying is that when you discern that someone is being hella Judasy, you can call an audible and veto that person.

> **You and your spouse should have veto power - the power to ban your spouse from seeing someone.**

Let me give you an example. I have a great circle of friends—both male and female. If Chris ever had a problem with one of my friends and felt that they were being detrimental to me or our family, he would have the right to ask me to stop seeing that person. As his wife, I need to honor his request—even if I disagreed with his assessment. Here's why: men understand other men and their motives in ways that women will never understand. Just like women can see things in other women that men will never see. Call it your Spidey-sense, intuition, wisdom, or whatever, but it's true. You have to respect your husband's vision just like you want him to respect yours.

Let's reverse it. Let's say your fiancé has a group of friends, and one of the women in the group is a bit too friendly. Nothing overt but she's just a bit too attentive to your future husband. You talk to him about it, but you can't really pinpoint what she is doing that makes you uncomfortable. You just know that you hear warning bells whenever she is around and know in your spirit that she is up to no good. Veto. VEEEEE-TOOO!

I am serious. Explain to your boo why she is getting vetoed and move on. Unless you really were bitten by a radioactive spider (shout out to Stan Lee!) that Spidey-sense is really the Holy Spirit informing you of danger up ahead. Listen to it.

But let me give you a bit of caution, too. Do not veto everyone under the sun. Like seriously. Save veto power for the true Judases that pop up. Don't be *that* wife that never lets her husband go anywhere with anyone. Don't be Shelby from *The Best Man*. Don't have your spouse in a vise grip, afraid to hang out and have fun. No one likes a Shelby.

Reflection

You've thought about your friends but have you thought about his? Well, it's time to think about his "boys."

1. Have you met all of your man's friends? Do you love some and hate others?
2. Does your love have any friends of the opposite sex? How do you feel about them?
3. Are there any friends who give you the heebie jeebies or make you uncomfortable?

You need to embrace his circle of friends too, just like you want him to embrace yours. Don't sequester yourself off and think that you only need just the two of you. Friends are necessary. Keep those bonds healthy and strong. Those friends will help prop you up when you need it and will cheer you on during all of your marriage milestones.

You know what? Tomorrow, call your bestie and talk about her life without mentioning anything about your upcoming wedding. Trust me on this one, she'd love to speak with you.

Neysa

7

Family Matters

So Ms. My-Last-Name-Is-Changing, are you keeping up?

I know I have covered so many things in these letters: friends, prayer, money, and having realistic expectations for your spouse. I know. It's a lot.

But there's more to talk about, and this next subject is, yet again, another heavy topic—family. When the wedding march plays and the doors of the church open, all you will see is your spouse's

> **When you got married, you gained more than a spouse; you gained an entire family.**

smiling face. You will only have eyes for him. The rest of the folks in the room will be a blur. But once the wedding high wears off, you will quickly become aware that you didn't just gain a spouse; you gained family.

A what?! Yep, an entire family. The good, the bad, the ugly, and the broke. You inherit it all the minute you say "I do." You also have to shake off any familial traditions and carve out new ones for your household. When you are upset with your boo, you can't go running back to Mommy and Daddy. A lot of baggage comes with that little gold ring, and you have to be strong enough to carry it all.

We are family

Let's think about your upcoming wedding day again. As each guest arrives, they are asked if they are in attendance for the bride or the groom and seated accordingly by the ushers or hostesses. This is how your marriage will start with an aisle way between your family and his. The reception starts the same way. Everyone at their assigned tables sitting separately. At the reception something miraculous happens once everyone eats, drinks, and the DJ starts spinning the tunes. Lines blur. People converse and have a good time. Your actual marriage should look more like the reception dance floor - everyone intermingled and doing *The Wobble*.

Your family is awesome, right? I mean *you* think so. Sure you dad talks too loud, or your cousin is a crackhead who steals, but they're not bad people. And they are family. More importantly, *your* family. If your beau loves you, then he is bound to love them, too, right? Nope. I am sure he thinks that his uncle who calls himself a "playa" is a cool cat. But when you see him, you get the heebie-jeebies. Now those are just two basic examples, but how do you make his family yours and your family his? You have to spend time with both families.

Transparent moment: this is really hard for my family. My hubs is from California, and I am from Kentucky, but we reside in Tennessee. Between jobs, kids, and life, our time spent with family is not the best. It is actually one of the things I hate about living out of state. When you live so far away, you can become a little island unto yourself. We also have not been as intentional as we need to be about spending time with our families. We are making up for that by working on incorporating more extended family time. But as I've said repeatedly, don't be like us...be better than us.

Spend time with your families. Attend reunions. Eat with cousins. Nurture your family. Send cards and make phone calls. Invest in your extended family. If you don't, you will forever be the awkward person in the room. Getting to know people takes time and is intentional. If you don't spend time with *his* family, they will never become *your* family, and vice versa. Another reason that you need to get to know both sides of the family is due to the wealth of information that can be learned from our ancestors. You just have to tap it. You know the quote that "no man is an island?" Well, no family is an island either. You have to spend time with your extended families.

Reflection

1. Look at your phone log for the past week. Which family members have you called and checked in with?
2. If you live outside the city, who do you see when you come back to visit? Are you overlooking anyone?
3. Does your family accept your upcoming wedding and your future spouse?
4. What about his family? Do you spend time with his family without your fiance' around?
5. Does he help cultivate a relationship between you and his family and do you do the same for him?

Think about your current relationship with your family and his. Your actions during this period determine how you are perceived. Are you a bridezilla and not including his family in the planning? Don't do it, Miss Celie! You do not want to hear about putting his mom in a chartreuse dress years later at your child's 5th birthday party! Start the spirit of collaboration now!

Leave and Cleave

In the first letters of this book, I shared the verse that most premarital counselors bring up, Ephesians 5:31: "For this reason a man will leave his father and mother and be united to his wife, and the two will become one flesh." Wait a minute! Didn't I just say that you are gaining a family? Yep, sure did. And now I am saying you have to leave the family? Right again. While you are gaining a family, you also have to keep them at a distance when it comes to your marriage. Isn't that a conundrum? Of course it is. Did you think marriage would be easy? Hahaha. Nope.

You are gaining family, but you can't let them be involved in your day to day decision making. You can't let them make decisions for your household. For me that was very hard. Of course I love my mom. More importantly, I trust my mom. I am *very close* to my mother, and her opinion matters to me (Hey, Mommy!). But I had to learn that what is normal for my household might be very different from what she would want for me. But how do you get there? Growing up, your family has their way of doing things. His family has their traditions. Some of them are big like how your family celebrates Christmas on Christmas Eve. Others are small like how his family eats breakfast together every morning. Chris and I have to define the Taylor household for ourselves. No one else can do it for us.

In the book, *Becoming A Couple of Destiny*, Bishop Joseph Walker III and Dr. Stephaine Walker share how they encountered the same discord at the beginning of their powerful marriage. He writes:

> In Louisiana, my parents raised my siblings and me a certain way. The boys in the house took care of the outside of the house, and the girls took care of the inside. When it came time to eat, the wives prepared their husbands' plates. That's what I grew up with in Louisiana. On the other hand, Stephaine grew up on the West Coast in a home where her father cooked and served the meal to the entire family.
>
> Can you imagine the collision on the way? I'm sitting at her pastor's house after church. After we pray, I sit down, assuming Stephanie is going to ask me what I want on my plate. She got her plate and commenced to going through the line placing food

on it without asking me what I wanted. I just sat, hoping that eventually she would ask me what I wanted. When it didn't come and instead I received a question of when I was going to fix my plate, I was stunned into reality. As funny as that is now, it was the beginning of a process of intentional merging of our different backgrounds in our new reality.

Can you imagine Bishop Walker sitting there, mouth set for a piece of fried chicken (He is a Baptist pastor, so it had to be fried chicken), and Dr. Stephaine comes back to the table with her plate full of food, sits down, and takes a bite. I bet he was heated! This may seem like a minor thing, but it is a great example on how family paradigms can set up your expectations in your marriage.

Reflection

Once you get married, you have to set up your own traditions. You have to find a way to make "his way" and "her way" transform into "our way."

1. What are your favorite family traditions?
2. Where do you expect to spend your holidays?
3. If you live far away from relatives, how often will you go to visit them?

Talk with your fiance' about these expectations now so that you can then speak to your parents about your plans. You don't want your families to assume that you will attend the July 4th BBQ and bring your strawberry cobbler if you know that you will not be in attendance. Let them know in advance that you can't make it while sharing which events you will be attending. It will help the news go smoother.

Family Feud

There is some news you shouldn't share with the 'rents. These are your disagreements. When you fight—and you will fight—please don't go running to your parents and tell them every horrible thing your hubby did. Guess who did that? Can you see me slowly raising my hand? Yep, me. Now I could try to justify it by saying that I didn't know better at the time (I really didn't), but the reality is that I didn't even think about anything beyond the fact that I was hurt and that my mommy had my back. Believe me—if you have Jesus and my mom on your side, then you can take on the world.

Let me put it differently. If someone does my siblings or my children wrong, then they have to suffer the Wrath of Neysa. Believe me when I say it is legendary. There is fire breathing and swordplay involved in this wrath. Once I have inflicted proper revenge on the assailant, I will give them the side-eye for years to come. Trust me when I tell you YEARS. So imagine how your parents feel when they see you hurt or upset over something your spouse did. They are your parents. They will always love you and think you are an angel. That is what parents are supposed to do. That is how parents are wired. So can you imagine a family dinner after you've told your parents that your fiancé hurt you in some way? The menu would be a roast and mashed potatoes, with a side of stalled conversation and icy cold stares. Awkward.

Parents have long memories. Parents can hold grudges. When you have prayed and moved on, they will still suck their teeth the moment your boo walks by. Parents are in your corner - always. So don't put yourself or them in a difficult position. Keep them out of your business.

Neysa E. Taylor

If you thought designing a reception seating chart keeping your drunk Uncle Charlie away from his church deaconess Auntie Renee was tough, the merging of families is even tougher. But it is only tough on the front end as everyone is learning their new roles and new expectations. The work you put in at the beginning pays off as you find support, love and acceptance that only family can give.

Welcome to the Fam!
Neysa

8

Forbidden Fruit

Hey, girl!

Ok, ok, I am about to tell you a joke. Now according to my kids and husband, I am not that funny so I am not going to tell you a Neysa-original joke which is really only a paraphrase of a joke told by well-known comedian, Sommore. The joke goes a bit like this: Imagine you are at an amusement park. You are riding all of the rides, but you see a big teddy bear that catches your eye. You desperately want that bear. So you quit riding the roller coasters and focus on winning the bear. And lo and behold, you win the bear. You love the bear, but now that you have the bear, you look around and realize that you can't get back on the roller coasters because you are carrying around a big bear. While Sommore tells this joke much more comedically than I do — I really am funny y'all — the gist is the same. Before you get married, you see dating as a playground, but once you get married and "win the bear," your love of dating doesn't just magically go away. Most people expect those feelings to just disappear. They don't. You are the same person with a wedding ring that you were without a ring.

When reading this, you may be thinking, "Here comes the letter about Chris's affair." Nope. Since I am writing this for a bride, I am going to talk about how I was tempted. Oh, the shock and awe. People's mouths are hanging open. And guess what? We are going to get to that, but let's first address the past –your exes.

Don't Look in the Rearview Mirror

Let's be honest. Most people aren't virgins when they get married. I know this is a spiritual-based book, but chances are you've had sex before. Am I right? Even if you are a virgin, you probably have been in relationships in the past, and trust me, emotional entanglement can be as problematic as a sexual encounter. But there are two things that you have to do to really move on from your exes — whether the relationships were sexual or not. First, you cannot romanticize your exes. Secondly, you have to pray for old memories to be erased.

Imagine you are driving down the street headed to a new destination. As long as the view ahead is beautiful, you are focused on where you are going. But let's say the road view is desolate and dry. You may make the mistake of looking in the rearview mirror. Looking in the rearview mirror doesn't get you any closer to your destination. If anything, it causes you to start second-

> **Don't compare your husband to anyone else, not even Idris Elba, Chris Hemsworth, or Jesse Williams.**

guessing where you are going and may even make you do a U-turn. This is even more important in your relationship. Let's say you are going through a tough patch in your relationship. You can start thinking, "I didn't have this problem with *insert-ex's-name-here.*" You may even start romanticizing your ex and your relationship with him. That doesn't serve you or your marriage. There is a reason your ex is your ex. Don't forget that. And don't compare your husband to anyone else. Not your past, not Idris, no one.

This is even more important when it comes to previous sexual encounters. In the book, *He-Motions,* Bishop T.D. Jakes says this of men: "We sometimes try to force all of the images we have of women onto the woman we're with now. But in order to come to a whole relationship, a balanced and strong union, we must exorcise these expectations and embrace the person who shares our bed." You have to never look in the rearview mirror when it comes to sex. Seriously. If you are focused on So-&-So did this or that better, you will never cultivate a healthy sex life with your spouse. Sex with your husband is special. It's a safe place to explore WHATEVER you want to explore sexually. Too often people think that they have to be sanctified in the bedroom. Puh-lease! Throw that thought out the door. Married sex should be the best, most thrilling sex of your life! (More on that will come in the next section. Trust me. You'll want to read that section.) But if you haven't embraced the freedom of married sex and are having a lackluster time, you may be reminiscing or fantasizing about a previous lover. Stop that. Like right now, stop that! That will only damage your marriage bed. So what should you do? You have to pray for the old memories to be erased. You have to ask for that desire to be removed. How can you learn to love sex with your hubs if you are always thinking about sex with your ex? How can your sexual appetite for your spouse grow if you are still satiated with the sex of your ex-boyfriend? It can't. You have to purge the craving for your ex before you can crave your husband.

So what if you are thinking, "This has nothing to do with me. My hubs is the best lover ever!" That's great! high five, sista girl! But still watch your back. Why? You have to stay on guard because temptation is real. It's really real. If you don't believe me, just keep reading.

Reflection

Take a moment and list all of your sexual partners. Write each name down. Now get rid of it. Tear it up, burn it, flush it down the toilet. No looking back. Now, let's look forward.

But I Like It

I am a great mom. I know what makes my children tick. I know what motivates them and what they don't like. So when I want to treat them or show them a little extra love, I don't say "Hey, who wants some broccoli?" Broccoli doesn't motivate them at all. But if I say, "Hey, who wants some ice cream?" Everyone's hands start waving in the air, right? Right. Now you may be thinking what does this have to do with temptation? Everything. Satan knows what you like and what you don't like. Satan knows that you prefer ice cream over broccoli. Trust me, he knows what you like, what you are curious about, and what will really tempt you.

As I mentioned before, the Bible says Satan comes to "steal, kill and destroy" (John 10:10). He is patient, he is cunning, and he is deliberate. He knows what you like and will gently dangle what you desire in front of you until you are salivating. Can I make it plain? If you like your men tall, dark, and handsome, it's no coincidence that your new coworker is tall, dark, and handsome. Why would Satan dangle something that you don't like in front of you? In other words, why would he dangle broccoli in front of you when he knows you love ice cream?

Another way Satan tempts you is by giving you whatever you are missing in your relationship. If you are fighting with your man about his lack of attention, then your new "friend" will be super attentive. If you are arguing with your hubs about his love of sports, your coworker will love spending time hanging out with you. When your spouse isn't listening, your male friend will always have a listening ear. That doesn't mean that every male in your life is bad. But you have to be on guard to keep it from slipping into the problem zone.

This is where I have to personalize it to make you understand that it can happen to anyone. I hate cheating. I loathe adultery. I've written blogs against it. All of that doesn't make me immune to temptation. Like "we fall down, but we get up" tempted. I could try to justify it and tell you I was in a dry place in my marriage. I wouldn't be lying. I really was in the desert and was sick and tired of being there. See, I believe in marriage. But I am human, and sometimes, you get tired of fighting for something that you don't see improving. I was there. Singing all of the Mary J. Blige "F him, girl" songs. And that was when I met a great guy. A really great attentive guy who loved Jesus and also loved him some Neysa. Was the guy, satan? Nope. But did the devil use my being in a dry place and this really nice guy to lure me away from my husband? Yep. Lure is probably too strong of a word. I wasn't some delicate flower who was overcome by vapors (Does that still happen? I don't think so). I vividly remember praying, "God, help me because I am about to slip." But I was praying and flirting. Instead of running from temptation, I kept flirting with it.

Playing with fire then wondering why I got burned. I knew better. I really did. Even though I knew better, I didn't do better. To be completely honest, I didn't *want* to do better. I wanted a break from my dry reality. I didn't want to fight for my marriage anymore. I wanted to be free to channel Olivia Pope and "walk in the sun."

No one tells you that "walking in the sun" has consequences (They do, girl, they do!). There is always a price to pay. You could lose your marriage. You could waste your purpose. You could throw away your destiny on something fleeting. And you are going to be tempted. Not once, not twice ,but every single day. Seriously. There are days when you are prayed up, and you will say, "Not today, Satan." Other days, when you are worn and battered, you may not see it coming. But if you start to notice yourself sliding down Temptation Road, hit the brakes immediately.

Reflection

This is definitely reflection time. How do you know if you are sliding down Temptation Road? Here are a few indicators:

1. Are you spending more time with the friend than your husband?
2. Are you deleting or hiding messages with your friend from your husband?
3. Are you comparing your husband to your friend?
4. Does the time with your friend seem easy compared to the hard times with your husband?
5. Do you smile when you get a text from your friend but roll your eyes when you get a text from your husband?

Trust me when I say this to you: RUN LIKE HELL! Run. Run fast amd run far! Put distance between you and the temptation. The friend may really be a great person. He may not be evil. But in your marriage, the improper relationship is definitely detrimental.

Right now, you may be thinking, "I love my fiancé. That will never happen to me." Ohh, ok. (Please note: that last comment was sarcastic, and I am giving you the side-eye right now) There will be a time when the sparkle of the honeymoon phase fades, when life-bills-kids take over your every moment, and you find yourself in a desert. Hear me well. When you walk into that season, pull out this letter and read it again. After you read it, follow these steps:

- Flee from temptation. Stop fueling the fire. If you were in the park and noticed the ground smouldering, you wouldn't pour gasoline on it, would you? No. So don't fuel temptation. The minute you notice it run away. Immediately.

- Do a critical analysis of your marriage. Is it a good marriage going through a rough patch? Is it a bad marriage? Seriously, look at your marriage with a critical eye. Ask yourself what is missing in your marriage that is causing another to catch your eye.

- Work on your marriage. In the book, *Greater*, Stephen Furtick mentions how you have to "burn the plow" to keep from going back to old ways (1 Kings 19:21). You have to stop investing in temptation and invest into your marriage. The grass isn't greener on the other side. The grass is green where it's watered.

Most importantly, don't slip, sis. Don't waste your time looking back or flirting with temptation. The repercussions of an indiscretion are long lasting, damaging, and far reaching. Don't blow your marriage on an affair. Don't do it, girl.

Be strong, my sister!
Neysa

9

Sexual Healing

Bride-to-be,

I know you just read that title of this letter and started singing a 'lil Marvin Gaye. If you didn't start singing "baaa-by, I'm hot just like an oven..." then I don't think we can keep on being friends. It's time to get down and dirty. The last letter was tough but we are diving in and talking about S-E-X. Yes, sex. Boom, chicka bow wow.

    Well actually only part of this letter is about sex. The other parts are about the precursor to sex - health and wellness. Marriage is until death do you part. Why would you want to spend 60+ years with someone that isn't keeping themselves up? Why would someone want to spend 60+ years with you if you aren't keeping yourself up? Physical fitness is important to your marriage. Of course you want to be sexually attractive to your partner, but you also want to be around to enjoy your partner for a long time.

Neysa E. Taylor

Health Is Wealth

This letter is likely to cause my primary care physician and my husband's oncologist to laugh. I have had nearly as many surgeries as I have fingers. My hubs has had cancer three times. We are NOT the poster children for great health. I could say that we are not in great health due to our jobs, kids, etc. But the honest answer is that we are like millions of other folks that take our health for granted and are lazy. You see how that is present tense? I wrote "take our health for granted" and not "took our health for granted." While I have been going to the gym at 4am, I can quickly slide into the wonderful world of carbs. It can happen at a moments notice. Again don't be like us. Be better than us.

Here is what we know to be true: More than one-third of all Americans are obese.[2] Due to this, obesity conditions like heart disease, stroke, type-2 diabetes, and certain types of cancer are running rampant. Facts don't scare us anymore. If they did, we would all be eating lettuce and running 5ks. But alas, we don't. So maybe we have to approach physical fitness differently.

What if we think about fitness as protecting those that we cherish the most? Most women tend to take better care of others than we do ourselves. So what if we played off of the need to protect others in our quest for health? Look, I know what you are thinking. We should want to be healthy for ourselves and not for others. I get it. But the reality of it is that hasn't worked for so many women who are overworked with no time to spare for themselves, and when

---

[2] https://www.cdc.gov/obesity/data/adult.html

we do get a moment, I would rather sit and watch *Scandal* with a large glass of wine than hit the treadmill. So, let's change the paradigm.

As I was saying, what if we thought of being physically fit as doing something for our family, which we just happen to reap the benefits from as well? Here's how it works: You work out because you don't want to be a liability to your family in the future. You want to raise your future kids and be around to teach them how to ride a bike. You want to do a cartwheel and hula hoop with your future daughters. You want to be able to walk on the sand hand in hand with your boo as you celebrate your 25th anniversary. To make all of this happen, you need to move your boo-tay.

Reflection

Let's get this health and wellness together.

1. Have you had a check up recently? Dental, physical, gynecological?
2. Do you make time for sufficient rest?
3. Are you managing your stress? Nothing is a bigger mood killer than stress.
4. Are you committed to some form of physical fitness?

And speaking of moving that boo-tay, there is another reason you should work up a sweat. So you can get sweaty horizontally as well. (Cue back up the Marvin Gaye).

Preserving the Sexy

News flash! Men are visual creatures. Another news flash — so are women! Remember when you first saw your fiancé?

Something attracted you to him. Maybe it was his smile or his biceps. It may be his amazing legs or tight booty. Before you spoke a word to him, there was something physically that caught your eye and your attention.

This attraction is even stronger for him. It could have been your eyes, hips, waist, or smile that first attracted him to you. Whatever it was, it made him not only notice you, but muster up the nerve to come speak to you. Look at where that physical attraction has brought you. Glance at that diamond on your left hand. You are engaged! That physical attraction is so easy right now. Everything is new, fresh, shiny, and wonderful! If I were a betting woman, I would bet $5 that you have been dieting and in the gym getting ready for that beautiful wedding dress. Brides work so hard to look perfect on their wedding day, but what about the next day or a year after? Most are no longer putting in work in the gym or just eating lettuce.

Yes, your man should love you no matter how you look. But most folks want a cutie on their arm. Good thing is, that cutie is defined by you, and love gives you rose-colored glasses to look at your boo-thang. That doesn't mean to let yourself go. You shouldn't present your best to the outside world and give you hubs the leftovers. I am not saying you need to be casket sharp all of the time, but let's not walk around looking like Freddy Krueger either. You can be comfy and cute.

> **Preserving the sexy means taking care of your health and paying attention to your personal grooming.**

Preserving the sexy means taking care of your health and paying attention to your personal grooming. I started this by saying men are visual creatures, remember? That means that you will have to shave the entire leg. You will have to trim the forbidden forest. You will invest in some sexy lingerie. Sistas, you will take that head wrap off before it is "busy" time. I know you spent three hours in the hair salon, but come on, your boo deserves to see you perform at your best. Also, if he messes your hair up, I bet he will pay to get it done again.

Reflection

Girlfriend, let's keep it real. Are you keeping it tight and right? Or have you put on love pounds—you know, those pounds you put on while hanging with your boo? I am not worried about those pounds and I am sure he isn't either. But what about the wrapping? Go through your laundry basket. Yes, it's dirty but go through it.

1. What have your worn recently? Granny panties? Stained tshirts?
2. Is there any lingerie in the basket?
3. Is your *around the house* wear disgusting?
4. Look at your feet. Are they koala bear feet that can climb trees or are they suckable toes? (What?! Don't be scared! We are all grown here.)

You plan to be married until death. That is a long time, and you want the playground equipment to be fully functional as long as possible. (Cue the Trey Songz. Yep, we are about to go deeper).

Your Body Is A Wonderland

While you should not be having sex with someone who is not yet your husband, let's just assume that you may have fallen short of that goal. Since you are already familiar with that ride, let's also assume that things were/or still are hot and heavy. That's great! You are loving on him, and he is loving on you. Frequently. Let's fast forward to after the rice has been thrown and your tan from your honeymoon has faded. Sex may slow down a bit. Look, life happens. We all get busy with trying to climb the corporate ladder or raise kids, but we have to have sex more often. You have to be in the mood more than on his birthday or your anniversary.

You also have to switch it up. My baby brother (he hates that title) is married to a wonderful woman. Before they jumped the broom, I let her in on a sexy little secret. Do you want to know the advice I gave my sister-in-law? I told her to consistently serve up B+ bedroom shenanigans. Not A+ but B+. I am sure you are scratching your head, wondering why, so let me explain. Imagine your favorite meal. For me it is an amazingly rare prime rib with garlic cheddar mashed potatoes and creamy horseradish sauce on the side. Yuuummm! What is your favorite meal? Visualize it. So what if I told you that is all you get to eat for the rest of your life? Initially you would think, "Wooo-hooo! I just hit the culinary lottery!" For approximately the first month, you are happy. But what about 60 days later? I bet you'd be tired of eating "your favorite meal." I am pretty sure that it is quickly changing from your favorite meal to food you never want to see again. After a year, you would want anything but your favorite food. You wouldn't even be able to stand looking at your favorite food.

Think about sex the same way. If you are doing your best tricks every day, then even your best tricks (yes, that one that makes him speak in tongues and curl up in a fetal position) will become lackluster for him. That's why I say give him B+ on a regular basis and punctuate it with A+ on his birthday, Easter, and random Tuesdays. Trust me!

Also, don't get stuck in a sexual rut. You both should always surprise each other. If you always do A, B, and C in that order, please switch it up. Learn something new. Add an "H" to your sexual alphabet. Take a moment and read an erotica book or two. Try to play "helicopter" with the ceiling fan. (Do you remember that old D.L. Hughley joke? I told you I was funny). Do naked yoga and see what happens. Play Twister nude. Go on a field trip to the Hustler store, and each of you buy one thing you want to try. Read *The Joy of Sex* or the *Kama Sutra*. Try one of the poses. Keep it lighthearted and fun. Remember, this is your spouse. If you got married at 30 and live to 90, that is 60 years of sex with that one person. That one person whom you love more than anyone else on the planet. The one person who can make your toes curl over and over again. So, try something different. If you like it, keep it as part of your sexual repertoire. If not, try something new the next night. This is how you keep him on his toes. Better yet, this is how you keep your toes curling.

So are you all hot and bothered yet? Well, cool off. Remember I said this is for the married folks. Start planning now on how you will blow his mind for years to come starting on your wedding night.

You aren't listening to me are you? You are probably already making plans with your man. Oh, well. Lord, I tried.

Get it, Get it!
Neysa

10

Expanding the Family Tree

Hey, Friend:

Right now you are a bride-to-be but have you ever thought that one day you might be a mama-to-be? By now you should be over being shocked by my personal questions. I mean, I just talked about B+ sex in the last letter. While you are thinking about recreation, we also need to talk about procreation: kids.

Chris and I had 1.5 kids when we got married. What?! Our oldest was in attendance, and our youngest daughter was the reason the wedding was moved up by two months. See, 1.5 kids in Neysa math. It's new math, like calculus and common core.

Maybe you have

> **Children are wonderfully, terrible beings. They fill your heart with love and deprive you of sleep.**

kids or maybe little crumb snatchers haven't crossed your mind yet, but if you are getting married (and I assume you are because you are reading this book), then you need to start thinking whether or not you want children and if you do, what that means for you both. Also, if you are reading and practicing the previous letter, you *really* need to start thinking about the role children may play in your lives.

Children are wonderfully, terrible beings. They fill your heart with love while keeping you up all night so that you are so sleep deprived and forget your own name. I love our kids, but I would be lying if I didn't say that parenthood is the most rewarding, yet hardest job ever. There are a million decisions that have to be made daily that affect the future of your child. Want to skip cooking tonight and just drink wine and eat cake icing? Nope, not if you have little ones at home. The CDC, the pediatrician, and children's services all say they need a balanced meal.

While the weight of the million decisions you have to make can seem overwhelming, there are a few big ones that you have to address head-on. The first is to commit to ending any negative family issues before you have children. The second is to get your life and wealth in order to bless your grandchildren. (Yes, grandchildren.) The third is to remember that you and your spouse are teammates. Let's jump into the first one.

End Generational Curses Now

I love my parents. I really do. But while I look like the perfect merger of their DNA, I didn't really think that I was really that much like them. I was wrong. I am just like my parents. When it comes to my sense of humor, mannerisms, and temper, I really am Clarence and Anne's child. When I look at my children, I see so much of Chris and I in each of them. Our oldest is an overachieving leader just like her mother. Baby girl is an artistic wunderkind—theatre, dance, singing, and music. She is a little ball of talent like Chris. Whenever they do something awesome, both of us swell with pride and beam a little brighter. We take credit for their achievements by saying, "Guess what *my* daughter did today."

However, when they do something not so great, our conversations start like this: "Guess what *your* child did today?" We don't want to claim the negative behavior. As awesome as the kids are, they also show you the other side of yourself. Children show you the best and the worst of who you are. That's right. Both sides of yourself are visible in your kids. Our oldest daughter is my mini-me, just like my youngest daughter is a mini-Chris. Daughter #1 is a tell-it-like-it is, type A, born leader personality. Good, right? Yes it is, but she is also short on grace and mercy, and her tongue is sharper than a Cutco knife. Daughter #2 has talent by the bucket. Sing, dance, act, draw, if it can be done on stage, she is good at it just like my husband. Those are awesome traits to have, but she wrestles with procrastination and motivation like her father. Your children have your DNA. They have your smile, your toes, your blessings, and unfortunately, your curses. You pass down more than just the good stuff. You can pass down curses, too.

Wait, curses? Yep, curses. The good news is that you can stop them, but first you have to recognize them, actively work against them, and warn your children about them.

Recognizing Curses

For a moment, think back over your life. Think about the times when you have really fallen short or had serious troubles. Now think back a generation about your parents. Did they make the same mistakes? What about your grandparents or great-grands? Do you see a pattern? Chances are you do. Are you having an "a-ha" moment? I know I did when I first started looking at parenting from a curses perspective. This doesn't mean that your parents or grandparents are bad people. It does mean the devil is patient and will prey on a family for years to try to thwart their blessings and purpose. So you have to recognize the pattern - not to be used as a crutch to justify your bad behavior but so that you can actively work against it.

Working Against Curses

So, you recognized a distinct pattern in your family. Now what? You better get to work. Think of it this way: imagine a murderer is in your house. You see him. You know his plan is to kill you. Do you just holler, "I see you," and keep on doing what you are doing? I hope not. If so, we are going to hear about your untimely death on the news tonight. Most folks would start *doing* something. Fight, throw something, look for a weapon, or run are all good answers for things to do when a murderer is in your presence. You use the same techniques when dealing with the enemy as well. You put distance between the curse and your life by praying, monitoring your behavior, making sure you never give him an inch because he will always take a mile and then some.

Warn the Future

Maybe you never touched an alcoholic beverage in your life because your parents were alcoholics. You refuse to be ruled by that curse. Great! Awesome step! You are probably going to pat yourself on the back and say, "I ended that curse." Let's jump ahead to your kids as teens. They attend a party and try alcohol. They like it. They like it so much that they start the spiral into alcoholism. So, did you really end the curse? Nope. Not because you didn't actively work against it—*you* did. You made decisions that kept it from ruling your life. The step you missed was warning the next generation so that they can keep guard as well.

Remember I told you the devil is patient. You can't forget about him lurking outside your door. I know that

> **The devil is patient. Don't. Give. Him. An. Opening.**

you didn't let him in, but he is still out there waiting for someone to give him an opening. Don't. Give. Him. An. Opening. Seriously, talk to your kids about familial struggles. I know that you don't want to share all of the family's business, so omit names if you need to, but talk to your kids. Pray over your kids. Correct your kids. Give them a fighting chance, too.

Neysa E. Taylor

My Beloved is Mine and I am His, But the Kids are Rented

In October 1999, I became a mother. When I looked down at this perfect little 5 pound 14 ounce baby, I knew that everything in my life had changed. Ev-er-y-thing! My days and nights revolved around my baby. In June 2002, I did it again. And once again, I was in love. Deep in love with this little girl that had captured my heart. Nothing mattered but them. Imagine my heartache in May 2017 when my baby — my 5lb 14oz baby — graduated high school and made plans to leave my home. Can you believe that my second born, the little heart snatcher that was born in 2002, plans to leave soon, too?

While I am wiping tears away, I know they were designed to leave. It's all part of the plan. You have children. You nurture them, and they leave. You must have faith that you've given them your best, but eventually they will fly away. After they leave the nest, guess what you are left with? Uh-huh, that's right, your spouse. Remember that person whom you virtually ignored for 18 years? Yep, he'll be standing there next to you. Now what? After a whole lifetime, the two of you might be virtually strangers. He kind of looks like a guy that you once knew. You are the woman that he used to find sexy. Chances are you haven't had a real conversation in years. Sure, you discuss school, work and bills, but I bet the two of you haven't discussed dreams in eons.

Now take a deep breath and put the crystal ball down. Remember, you are a fiancée. You haven't had kids yet or at least you aren't so far gone that you can't turn it around. How do you keep your spouse from becoming a stranger? Keep the newness in your marriage. Keep the sense of wonder in your marriage. Keep dating your spouse. Invest in your spouse and keep it fresh. Fresh means you have to always try new things. Concerts, restaurants, workouts, dancing, sporting events, festivals, pizza joints, tattoo shops, and etc. You cannot continue to do the same thing over and over. Believe me when I tell you that it is easy to get into a rut once you have kids. You work 40+ hours a week, come home to kids' sporting events and homework, fix dinner, and discuss who paid what before you turn in just to do it all over again. On a good night, the family will go to O'Charley's or the Sizzler for dinner, and you might get a poke and a tickle (that means sex y'all) before you fall asleep. There is nothing wrong the Sizzler. I love the cheese bread, but 18 years of Sizzler is boring. You have to spend time together still seeing the world and each other through fresh eyes. This is how you sustain your marriage and don't end up strangers.

Reflection

Remember that list you made after the *Surviving the Storms* letter. Pull it back out. Pull your calendar out too. Evaluate your schedule and finances and ask yourself the following questions:

1. How often can you accommodate a real, outside-the-house, date night?
2. What is your non-negotiable couples thing? Do you have a game night? Dancing? Listen to live music? Do you work out together every Thursday? What is the thing that you do that you never miss?

You have to be intentional about adult time even as you are raising children.

Neysa E. Taylor

Blessing to My Children's Children

Did I mention that I am not the best at money management? I think I mentioned that in a previous letter. And you've heard that having a kid is expensive, right? Yep. According to the Department of Agriculture, it is over $200-thousand dollars.[3] Um-hmm, that is U.S. dollars. And that only gets you to age 18. What about college? What about books, a car, hair weave/extensions, spring break trips? I know those are first-world problems, but since I live in the first world, those are my problems. So if $200k isn't enough, what I am expected to leave something for my grandchildren? You are sitting there thinking "how did we get onto grandkids? I don't even have kids yet." Let me pull out my Bible and show you. The Word says in Proverbs 13:22, "A good man leaves an inheritance for his children's children..." Yep, that's what it says, so start saving those coins.

    Let me introduce you to my father-in-law. Mr. Taylor is the epitome of this verse. My daughters know that Pa-Pa has their back. In fact, he often says, "Shoot, I can't take it with me." Pa-Pa believes in family and taking care of them. He knows that his legacy is rooted in his offspring—his children and his grandchildren. Seeing them well cared for and prospering makes him feel good. This is different from spoiling although he does spoil his grandchildren. But he *cares* for them. He is the epitome of Proverbs 13:22. His care for others doesn't stop at his grandchildren. Mr. Taylor is invested in his family. In a society where Black men are erroneously viewed as deadbeat, Mr. Taylor's commitment to family shines in the shadow of that stereotype. I can't even begin to count the number of family members that Mr.

---

[3] http://time.com/money/4629700/child-raising-cost-department-of-agriculture-report/

Taylor has supported or raised. I really can't count them because his reach is just that vast.

While Pa-Pa's financial support is amazing, I want you to understand that *he* is the blessing not the money. Yes, the finances are a part of that, but Mr. Taylor's love and example of agape[4] love is the real blessing that will be passed on to future generations.

I know this letter was heavy. You just received an engagement ring and here I am talking about kids, grandkids, and still having time for a date night. It's a lot to handle but being about the Kingdom building business is serious work. Marriages become families and families become generations. The time and attention you put into preparing for marriage will ripple throughout future generations. While it is serious, it's work that I assume you want to do. No one looks back and says "I am so proud that I messed up my great-grandkids." Everyone I've ever met wants their kids to be better off then they are. The problem is that people aren't being cognizant nor intentional about their actions. People expect success in school to take work. Success in business takes a plan and execution of said plan. Success in marriage and in turn a family, doesn't just happen by chance. You have to plan for it. Girl, get your pencil and paper ready for what's coming next.

Neysa

---

[4] Agape is the Greek term for the highest form of love. This love is unconditional and sacrificial.

11

Write the Vision and Make It Plain

Pat yourself on the back, Little Miss Bride-to-Be. You have made the journey through this book. Can you believe that you will soon be Mrs.?

We've discussed accepting your spouse as they are right now. We've delved into temptation and resisting it. We've talked about preserving the sexy and getting your freak on. You are prayed up and ready to put on that white dress... but like every good infomercial says, "But wait, there's more."

Habakkuk 2:2 reads, "Then the Lord replied: 'Write down the vision and make it plain on tablets so that a herald may run with it'." The vision has many names. Vision board, business plan, to-do list, etc. They all have one thing in common - they are a plan for you to follow for success. I know you want success in your marriage. So plan for it.

Marriage is an investment. You are investing your time, your energy, and your life to building a marriage with someone. You get *married* on a given date, but you build a *marriage*. It can only be built brick by brick. If you've ever built a house, you know that you have to have a blueprint for your home before you start to gather your tools. (See I'm back to engineering analogies. I told you, they just work). The same is true for your marriage. You and your fiancé need to create a blueprint for your family.

"Do You Know Where You're Going To..."

Have you seen the movie *Mahogany* with Diana Ross and Billy Dee Williams? You know, the one where she is a designer and model? I hope you have because that movie is EVERYTHING. I love that movie, and while it has nothing to do with marriage, there is a song that Ms. Ross performs on the soundtrack that speaks to having a blueprint for your family. She sings:

> Do you know where you're going to?
> Do you like the things that life is showing you?
> Where are you going to, do you know?
> Do you get what you're hoping for?
> When you look behind you there's no open door.
> What are you hoping for, do you know?

"What are you hoping for?" You are getting married, but what are you hoping for your marriage? If you have no expectations, then you are like a kindergartener at snack time--"you get what you get, and you don't throw a fit." But you are not a kindergartener. You are an adult. A grown-ass woman who is about to become someone's wife and, in the future, someone's mother. You can't leave your life up to chance.

I often tell my family that they are the author and the main character of their lives. This dual role puts them in charge of creating their own story however they see fit. But too many people live their lives like supporting cast members. We are not SIMS. No one is going to design a life for us to live. We have to listen to our hearts and our wildest desires because that is where our fullest lives lie.

> **You are the author and the main character of your story. Write something amazing for your family.**

How do you find out where you want to go? It's easy. Just describe your perfect life. I'm serious, describe it in detail. I mean in intricate details. In my perfect life description, I know how much I want to weigh, how my hair looks, and how often I work out. Ask your boo-thang to do the same.

I know it sounds all new agey but it works. Have you ever been to a vision board party? You know where you cut out pictures and words from magazines and glue them onto poster boards so you can envision your future? This is similar but with words. How can you achieve something you haven't first seen? You can't. Write the future you want to see.

Once you and your future husband write down your idea of perfection, you have to share your visions with each other. Talk about them. Ask questions. Lie in bed and visualize them. Then take the time to weave them together by creating a family vision. The live you both craft is your goal, your union's destination. You wouldn't go on vacation without discussing destinations, would you? If you didn't talk about where you wanted to vacay, one of you could end up wearing snow skis and the other packing a bikini. Those things do not mesh. By talking it out you get to determine if you are both headed in the same direction.

Reflection

I told you to grab your pen and paper. Also grab your lover. It's time to put them all to use.

1. Separately, write out how you want your life to be. Be descriptive.
2. If you find that too hard to do, write backwards. Not z, y, x backwards, but write your obituary. Sometimes you have to start at the end and work your way back.
3. Exchange papers and review them. Are there similarities? Glaring differences?
4. Work on merging both of those documents into one that you both agree on.
5. Finally, make a list of goals, a bucket list of sorts.

For the commitment-phobes out there, don't worry. (Side note: if you are a commitment-phobe, you probably shouldn't be getting married, but that is a whole 'nother conversation.) This is *your* plan. There are no wrong answers. Remember I told you that you don't turn it into anyone except your spouse. The only opinions that matters are yours and his. While I believe in reading your plan often to make sure you are on track, I also recommend reevaluating the plan yearly. Is that where you still want to go? If not, write a new plan. Remember if you are the author of your story, you are also in charge of revisions and edits. It's your life, your vision. Your perfection *together*.

What is Your Family's Mission Statement?

You're probably sayin, "What? A mission statement?!" Yep. What is the foundation for the family? Many organizations and businesses have mission statements to remind themselves and inform others about their purpose. At the church I attend, the entire congregation recites the mission statement each and every Sunday. In my day job – y'all know I do have a day job, right? - my organization's mission statement is everywhere. It's on every desk, office wall, publication, and it's recited daily. Every employee is indoctrinated in the mission of the organization. In meetings, it is not uncommon to hear someone ask how a particular decision supports the mission. Your family needs a mission statement as well. The blog, *The Art of Manliness*[5], explains it this way:

> For this reason, you may never have contemplated the question of *why*. Why get married? Why have a family? The importance of each individual having a clear purpose is often stressed these days, but few of us will travel this life alone. We'll make our way through the world as part of a family. Thus it is not enough to know your own purpose - who you are and where you are going. You must also determine the purpose of your family unit. Why does it exist, what does it stand for, and where are you going, *together*?

---

[5] http://www.artofmanliness.com/2013/08/21/creating-a-family-culture-how-and-why-to-create-a-family-mission-statement/

See your idea of perfection is the destination, the mission is your *who* and your *why*. "Who" speaks to who you are. The "Why" is really why you are a family. Stephen Covey states that "A family mission statement is a combined, unified expression from all family members of what your family is all about."

The Taylor Family's mission statement reads:

The Taylor Family is a six-person family created to love and support each other in the pursuit of our dreams both individual and collective. We will extend grace and mercy that allows one to make mistakes without being treated as a failure. We are blessed, thankful and will always value family over the world."

Short.
Succinct.
Ours.

Reflection

I suppose you know what I am going to ask you to do, right?

Sit down with your almost-husband and write your family's mission statement. This is your North Star. It should remind you of your commitment every single day.

Over Communicate to Reinforce the Vision

So, you've done the work. You've written the mission statement. You've crafted your perfect life. Done and done. Ummm, nope. Not quite. Why write it down and put it in a journal that you never open or refer to? Your mission statement is not an exercise or a bit of homework. Your mission statement has to become your lifestyle.

Matthew 5:15 says "Neither do people light a lamp and put it under a bowl. Instead they put it on its stand, and it gives light to everyone in the house." Your mission statement must give light to the entire house. My bathroom mirror is the most filthy item in my house. Why? My mirror is dirty because I am constantly writing on it with a dry erase marker. I track my weight loss (or gain) on the mirror. I have inspirational quotes on that mirror. I have a list of bills to be paid on there as well. I write on the mirror because I know I will look into it every day, multiple times a day. Where is your spot? Better yet, where is the family's spot?

Our family mission statement is on the kitchen wall. I posted it in the heart of the house to remind us of the Taylor plan. Our oldest child thought it was weird. Honestly, she gave it the serious side-eye when it was first posted, but now it is part of our world. It became part of our lifestyle.

Sis, you and your love have to craft your own roadmap for marriage. All the previous letters gave you tools but here is where you apply those tools and be intentional about your future together.

1. Visualize your future in detail.
2. Use a mission statement to hone your intention.
3. Over-communicate your mission by displaying it prominently in your home.

Does the vision seem "plain" to you now? I hope so because I want to see you win at wife-dom and kingdom building.

You are almost at the altar,
Neysa

12

What's Next?

Hey, Future Mrs. So-and-so,

You don't know this, but it took me forever to write this book. For-ev-er. Tiffany celebrated her one-year anniversary before I finished these letters. I think I am a good writer, but I never said I was a fast writer. But that's ok. You are getting my best tidbits; my lessons learned.

I also never professed to have a perfect marriage because what is perfect for one couple may not be perfect for another. But I wrote these letters with the hope that they help you avoid some of the mistakes that Chris and I have made (and repeated). Learn from my pitfalls and stumbling in the dark. What kind of friend would I be if I didn't shine a light for someone to follow?

You've read these letters, and you have — hopefully — reflected on each of them. It is only right to wrap them all up and give you my takeaways from each letter. Feel free to create a note card for each and keep them close by for quick reference.

1. Proverbs 31 - The Standard for a Woman of God

Engagement is a time of preparation. You must start preparing now for the future. You are now laying the foundation for your marriage.

2. Clark Kent v. Superman

Your spouse is not a fixer upper. Love him for who he is now, not who you want him to be. While you are loving him in his now, be prepared for him to evolve and change.

3. Dollars and Cents-ability

Money matters, so use business principles to mind your *personal* business. Be transparent and work together to mind your finances.

4. Praise and Worship

Get to know God for yourself. Invest in this relationship every single day. As each of you grows closer to God, the closer you'll become.

5. Learning to Survive the Storms

Problems are going to come, but when problems arise, work together to attack the problem, not each other.

6. Circle of Friends

Not every facebook friend is a true friend. Use discernment in determining who can be trusted with information regarding your marriage. Trust each other's intuition about your friends, and use veto power sparingly.

7. Family Matters

Marriage unifies two families not just two people. While your family shapes your outlook on marriage, you have to "leave and cleave." Be mindful of how much you share with your families about your relationship.

8. Forbidden Fruit

Don't look in the rearview mirror at past relationships. Be aware of temptation's pitfalls. Watch your back, my friend, watch your back.

9. Sexual Healing

I should write that you should protect your health (and you should), but if I am being honest, have sex. Have lots of open, honest, hot, freaky-deaky sex.

10. Expanding the Family Tree

Look for generational patterns and end curses before you have kids. Protect your legacy and create positive ripples throughout future generations.

11. Write the Vision and Make It Plain

Create a vision for your family and over-communicate the plan. Work together to achieve the life you have envisioned.

12. What's Next?

Define your marriage for yourself. If you want to have a rule where you eat pancakes naked on Saturday mornings, then do it. Seriously. This is your marriage.

Take my twelve letters and make them yours. Enjoy your marriage. Love your husband. Revel in your new season as wife.

Love,
Neysa

P.S. Oh, in case you were wondering, Tiffany was a lovely bride and has been an even more beautiful wife.

Acknowledgments

"Why aren't you writing?"
"You should really write more."
"Neysa, what are you waiting for?"

My village is awesome and encouraged/hounded me tirelessly. They believed in me when I didn't believe in myself. My loudest and most supportive cheerleader is my mom C. Anne Ellery. Everyone should have a mom like mine; the world would truly be a better place. Her love and support has given me wings. When I doubted myself, she was the wind on which I could fly. When I mentioned that I really loved writing, she purchased me a laptop so I could write on the go. Whenever my wings are battered, she happily loans me hers. My mother is amazing. Thank you, God, for gracing me with an awesome soror, friend, and mom.

To my children, Asyen, Maya, Preston, and Patrick: You. Are. Loved. Through it all, you bring me joy and make me want to be better to be a better mom, woman, friend, mentor, mom-mom, and person. I am so proud of you all, and I hope you can be proud of me, too. I can't wait to see who you become.

To my family - daddy (Clarence Ellery), Chris Michael, Tyson and Candice, Leonard and Johnetta Taylor, Dani and Timothy, Travis and Keisha, Sherri, Faith, the extended

Taylor family, the Brewers, Wrights, Gaines, Hayes, Ellerys, and the Bunko group (I really feel like I should just yell "502 Stand Up!"), I love you all and thank you for loving me.

To my entire sister circle: I am not going to list names because I will definitely leave someone out—thank you. I have the best group of women surrounding me, and I don't take it for granted. You are amazing. May we all be Wonder Women.

Keri, Tiffany, Carolyn—this labor of love is a testament to you all. Thank you for being my friend. Keri, one day I am going to lie to you just to see if you can detect it. Our nonverbal conversations speak volumes. Please never write my unauthorized biography and have it made into a Lifetime movie, but if you do, I want Kat Graham to play me. Tiffany, maybe since I've titled a book after you, you will stop giving me your legendary side-eye. Thank you for being my muse! Cool Carol, thank you for your words at brunch. Thank you for bringing me to tears with laughter whenever we are together. And thank you for listening to God when He told you to "gather" me and help me get my life. I hope you are proud.

To Tracey Michae'l Lewis-Giggetts, author and founder of New Season Books and Media, the way this has come full circle illustrates that God doesn't make mistakes and his time is not ours. Thank you for trusting me as a writer and transforming me into an author.

And finally to my husband Christopher Taylor: what more can I say about our love that is fit for print? Thank you for holding my hand and my heart; for forgiving me and accepting my forgiveness. Thank you for learning with me, encouraging me, and for allowing me to lay our marriage on the altar for the world to see. No matter what, you are always the place I call home. You are the Dewayne to my Whitley. #HBCULove I love you.

My Prayer

God,

Thank You for not giving up on me. Thank You for the lessons learned and the lessons to come. Thank You for You.

I know this was a long time coming, and I finally finished the assignment. It took me forever to get out of my own way and quit running from Your plan. I really hope You are proud of me.

So, what do You want me to do next?

~ me

www.ingramcontent.com/pod-product-compliance
Lightning Source LLC
Chambersburg PA
CBHW072053290426
44110CB00014B/1664